MW00564584

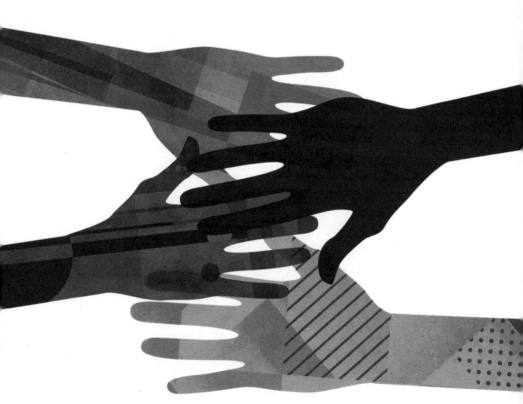

Praise for
No More Teaching Without Positive Relationships

"This vital resource reminds us that the work of teaching and learning is fundamentally human work: relational, social, and cultural. With a rare and necessary balance of personal, practical, and political, the authors support us in nurturing the kinds of anti-oppressive relationships with and among young people that make schools healthy, just, joyful, and successful."

—Carla Shalaby, author of *Troublemakers: Lessons in Freedom from Young Children at School*

"Through the voices of those closest to the classroom, Howard, Milner-McCall, and Howard remind us that at the end of the day, teaching and learning often boils down to caring relationships. While it is troubling that the field must be reminded of this fact yet again, until our most wounded children experience school cultures that prioritize their well-being over their test scores, we need the kinds of powerful voices represented in this book to keep the focus where it belongs."

—Jeff Duncan-Andrade, Associate Professor of Raza Studies and Education, San Francisco State University

Praise for
No More Teaching Without Positive Relationships

"This book should be on every educator's shelf and in every pre-service teacher's toolkit. This book is clear and concise yet complete."

—Maisha T. Winn, Faculty Director and Co-Founder of the Transformative Justice in Education Center, University of California, Davis

"Establishing and sustaining meaningful relationships with diverse learners is an increasingly urgent task for education practitioners. No More Teaching Without Positive Relationships *offers sound instruction for how to make subtle shifts in language and teaching disposition that enable favorable student outcomes. More than a one-size-fits-all 'how-to' guide of relationship-building, Howard and his colleagues draw on expertise in critical race studies, early childhood, and human development to forecast a vision of teaching and learning centered on more humanizing social relations."*

—Chezare A. Warren, Associate Professor of Urban Education and Teacher Education, Michigan State University

No More
Teaching Without
Positive Relationships

Dear Readers,

Much like the diet phenomenon Eat This, Not That, this series aims to replace some existing practices with approaches that are more effective—healthier, if you will—for our students. We hope to draw attention to practices that have little support in research or professional wisdom and offer alternatives that have greater support. Each text is collaboratively written by authors representing research and practice. Section 1 offers practitioner perspective(s) on a practice in need of replacing and helps us understand the challenges, temptations, and misunderstandings that have led us to this ineffective approach. Section 2 provides researcher perspective(s) on the lack of research to support the ineffective practice(s), and reviews research supporting better approaches. In Section 3, the author(s) representing practitioner perspective(s) give detailed descriptions of how to implement these better practices. By the end of each book, you will understand both what not to do, and what to do, to improve student learning.

It takes courage to question one's own practice—to shift away from what you may have seen throughout your years in education and toward something new that you may have seen few, if any, colleagues use. We applaud you for demonstrating that courage and wish you the very best in your journey from this to that.

Best wishes,
—*Nell K. Duke* and *M. Colleen Cruz, Series Editors*

NOT THIS BUT THAT

No More
Teaching Without
Positive Relationships

JALEEL R. HOWARD, TANYA MILNER-McCALL,
TYRONE C. HOWARD

HEINEMANN
PORTSMOUTH, NH

Heinemann
361 Hanover Street
Portsmouth, NH 03801–3912
www.heinemann.com

Offices and agents throughout the world

© 2020 by Jaleel R. Howard, Tanya Milner-McCall, Tyrone C. Howard

All rights reserved. No part of this book may be reproduced in any form or by any electronic or mechanical means, including information storage and retrieval systems, without permission in writing from the publisher, except by a reviewer, who may quote brief passages in a review.

Heinemann's authors have devoted their entire careers to developing the unique content in their works, and their written expression is protected by copyright law. We respectfully ask that you do not adapt, reuse, or copy anything on third-party (whether for-profit or not-for-profit) lesson-sharing websites.

—Heinemann Publishers

"Dedicated to Teachers" is a trademark of Greenwood Publishing Group, Inc.

The authors and publisher wish to thank those who have generously given permission to reprint borrowed material:

Figure 3.1 from *Choice Words: How Our Language Affects Children's Learning* by Peter Johnston. Copyright © 2003 by Peter Johnston. Reprinted with permission from Stenhouse Publishers. www.stenhouse.com

Library of Congress Cataloging-in-Publication Data
Names: Howard, Jaleel R., author. | Milner-McCall, Tanya, author. | Howard,
  Tyrone C. (Tyrone Caldwell), author.
Title: No more teaching without positive relationships / Jaleel R. Howard,
  Tanya Milner-McCall, Tyrone C. Howard.
Description: Portsmouth, NH : Heinemann, 2020. | Includes bibliographical references.
Identifiers: LCCN 2019049746 | ISBN 9780325118130 (paperback)
Subjects: LCSH: Teacher-student relationships. | Educational psychology.
Classification: LCC LB1033 .H695 2020 | DDC 371.102/3—dc23
LC record available at https://lccn.loc.gov/2019049746

Series Editors: Nell K. Duke *and* M. Colleen Cruz
Editor: Margaret LaRaia
Production Editor: Kimberly Capriola
Cover and Interior Designer: Monica Ann Crigler
Typesetter: Valerie Levy, Drawing Board Studios
Manufacturing: Val Cooper

Printed in the United States of America on acid-free paper

1 2 3 4 5 6 7 8 9 10 VP 25 24 23 22 21 20
January 2020 Printing

Dedicated to

*All my students who
demanded more of me
than my content knowledge.*

—Jaleel

*My parents, Henry and Barbara Milner, and
my brother Dr. Rich Milner, who are my biggest
supporters; my husband, Derek, and my children,
Ieshia, Byron, and Xavier, who encouraged me
throughout this process; and my students who
encouraged me to be a better teacher.*

—Tanya

*Jabari, Jameelah, Jaleel, and Jahlani: the four
individuals who have inspired me more than
anyone to create a more just, humane,
caring, and loving society.*

—Tyrone

CONTENTS

INTRODUCTION

Nell K. Duke

*I*n fourth grade, I sat on a plate of frosted cookies. I had put the cookies on my chair while I went to get a drink and when I returned, I sat right down on them. I was forever doing things like that, as my head was way up in a very nerdy version of the clouds quite a lot of the time. My teacher, Mrs. Quinn, responded instantly in a way that veered my own response away from tears and toward a feeling of being adored by her just for being my quirky little self. Her response set the tone for the rest of the class too—not "What is wrong with that girl!?" but "Oh sweet Nellie, we are so lucky to have her to lighten our day!"

Relationships matter. My relationship with Mrs. Quinn that year turned around what had already become a view of school as harsh, boring, and just not the place for me. I remember feeling like I learned a lot that year, but I know now that it was in no small part due to being in an environment in which relationships enabled me to learn. Many of you can look back on relationships with teachers that fostered learning; in fact, your memory of the relationships likely outlasts the details of the content you learned.
In practice, teacher-student relationships feel under threat. We have so much to teach in so little time; where is the time to build relationships? We need to know so much about students' achievement data; where is the space to know other things about them? We see students so enmeshed with their friends, their home lives, their phones, their fidget spinners; where is the space for us? And do we need to worry about knowing too much, being too friendly, sharing too much of ourselves?

This increasingly challenging climate for teacher-student relationships is juxtaposed with burgeoning research on the power of teacher-student relationships. Studies from so many angles—the association of teacher-student relationships with students' academic growth, the effect of having the same teacher multiple years, the role of race in teacher-student relations, and on and on—converge toward the fundamental conclusion that relationships matter. They can facilitate or undermine the success of our students.

No researcher in the field captures the importance of positive teacher-student relationships better than Tyrone C. Howard. Just hearing a presentation in which Dr. Howard related the simple act of correctly pronouncing students' names to a wide body of research and theory had me hooked on his approach to the topic of teacher-student relationships—an approach that reflects both an intimate knowledge of K–12 schools and a deep knowledge of theory and research. It is trite to say that something should be required reading; but Dr. Howard's review of research in Section 2 of this book *should be required reading.*

Jaleel Howard and Tanya Milner-McCall have taken an understanding of the power of teacher-student relationships and run with it. They help us see what it looks like in today's schools to form and continually develop relationships with students. They offer concrete practices—what we can do on Monday morning, literally—that we can enact in service of our long-term relational goals. They address head-on issues that arise, such as what constitutes oversharing, how to handle social media, and how to make room for relationships while ensuring that we continue to attend to developing academic skills. Their Section 3 covers a lot of ground, but you will be glad to walk there.

This is a book we need at a time we need it. I am so grateful to the authors, and to you, for engaging with this work. Students' hopes, their dreams . . . without positive teacher-student relationships, cookies are not the only things that can be crushed.

SECTION **1**

NOT ● THIS

"There Is No Time for Me to Have a Relationship with Every Student"

JALEEL R. HOWARD, TANYA MILNER-McCALL, TYRONE C. HOWARD

"I am so overwhelmed with all I have to teach."

"I have too many students and not enough time to build relationships with all of them. I am just not going to reach every student in class."

"I am not equipped to handle all the problems that students have."

"I just do not get these kids."

"My relationships with my students are good enough."

As teachers, we have heard, said, or thought each of these state-ments. Many more than once. We know most teachers want strong relationships with every student, but our limited time can make relationship-building feel challenging. There are so many things that demand our time and attention as educators and distract even the best of teachers from building individual relationships with students. As teachers like you, we know how relentless a school day, week, and year can be. Every day can feel like a battle between what we hope to accomplish and the interruptions that prevent us from achieving what we want. And, let us be honest, no one is holding us accountable for our relationships with students, but they are holding us accountable for academic results. So, we prioritize academic achievement and tell ourselves that is the best legacy of our teaching.

> For simple, quick strategies to build relationships with your students, see Section 3, pages 50–51.

Although ensuring students' academic achievement is an essential part of our job, it is not all of it. And although we are responsible for students leaving our class with transferrable skills and knowledge, are we grounding those skills and academic knowledge in authentic relationships so that students see how those skills and academic knowledge facilitate a successful, fulfilled, and joyful life? Are we prioritizing covering so much content over connecting with every student? We know firsthand how necessary it can feel to make that decision, but is it the right one?

As Tyrone will explain in Section 2, significant learning really cannot happen without a strong, positive relationship between the teacher and student: "Knowledge has to be communal, an experience, and relatable and transferrable to people" (Love 2019). When we do not build deep relationships with students, we decrease the effectiveness of our academic teaching.

"Knowledge has to be communal, an experience, and relatable and transferrable to people" (Love 2019).

To teach through our relationships with students, we need to shift from a rewards/punishment model—also known as a transactional model of teaching—to a relational or transformational teaching model that focuses on listening, learning, caring, and collaboration. Letting go of a rewards/punishment model of teaching can be difficult when we know that not learning academic skills and behaviors has real-life consequences for students. When teachers do not hold themselves accountable for students' learning, students pass from grade to grade without the knowledge they need, falling farther and farther behind high school graduation expectations and decreasing their likelihood of graduating. According to the Alliance for Excellence in Education (n.d.), "High school dropouts are nearly three times more likely to be unemployed than college graduates. Even when employed, high school dropouts earn about $8,000 a year less than high school graduates and approximately $26,500 a year less than college graduates." For Women and People of Color, these disparities in education and income are even more alarming. These are real consequences for our students' quality of life affecting everything from housing stability to health care access. It is easy to see how the best-intentioned teachers become singularly focused on covering content. But when we make that decision, we start to make more compromises. We prioritize covering content over reaching students, operating by a sense of urgency that can allow us to decide to focus on students who are the most likely to succeed over the success of all. Every teacher we know has had moments in their career where they have made that decision. When a student becomes consistently challenging, that student tends to be relegated as an outsider to our learning community, invisible, or merely a distraction. At times, successful learning and deep relationships with all students might feel like too much to accomplish, but we can. As an anonymous but often quoted line goes, "Students do not care how much you know until they know how much you care." This kind of caring, relational teaching often involves learning a different model than what we were taught. When we focus on teaching without relationships, we are making our job harder, and in some instances close to impossible.

"I am doing everything I can" is an important moment. But it is a moment of feeling rather than truth.

Sections 2 and 3 will provide you with research-based evidence and strategies to make both possible in your own classroom. But let us first acknowledge the struggle that happens in some teacher-student relationships.

Relationships are not easy. It often feels easier to walk away from a difficult relationship than to work through the difficulty. We have lived those moments in our teaching, and we know that you as the teacher-reader have, too. So, we would like to share some experiences from our classrooms that reflect moments when it is easy to give up. It is important to sit with the struggle for a minute rather than promise you this will be easy work. It will not always be easy. What we can promise you is that over time your teaching will be easier and more effective when you prioritize your relationships with students.

"I Am Doing Everything I Can"

In each example, we share a moment when we felt we had done everything we could to improve a teacher-student relationship. "I am doing everything I can" is an important moment. But it is a moment of feeling rather than truth. That feeling comes from one moment in time when we feel that we have no other resources or approaches to address a situation. That feeling can become a decision that describes our future commitment to a teacher-student relationship or it can be a decision to give ourselves time to reflect and gather the resources we need to make the relationship better. As you read these examples from our relationships with students, you might have already lived through and solved a similar challenge, you might be struggling in a similar scenario, or you might have different ones of your own. The point is to use these to reflect on the fact that *every* teacher has had experiences like these. There is no shame in feeling this way; it is essential to acknowledge the difficulty, as Tanya demonstrates in her classroom reflection.

From Tanya's Classroom

"This Student Gets in the Way of My Teaching"

I was warned about David before the school year even started. Teachers told me he was intelligent, but aggressive and disruptive. Despite their warnings, I began the school year confident that David and I would have a good relationship. At least once during both school breakfast and lunch, I made sure we had regular positive conversations. But David started to fulfill his past teachers' predictions, inter-

To see how Tanya worked to improve her relationship with David, see Section 3, page 81.

rupting class discussions by demeaning his peers, me, and the content. During independent work time, he would walk around the room and intentionally distract students who were on task. In our conversations, David showed that he understood why his behaviors were wrong but had little to no interest in improving. My confidence soon became frustration. Assigning him classroom jobs turned into an opportunity to disrupt the class and draw attention to himself. Positive rewards for good behavior would only work for a short period of time, no more than two days, and he would be back to the same old behavior with me more frustrated than before. Negative consequences did not work either. Keeping him in for recess only made his behavior worse after recess. He wanted to be able to do as he pleased in my classroom regardless of the rules, and he would often walk out when he did not get his way. Several times, he got physical with me and was removed from class. I had to call his father several times before we finally met in person. We discussed the fact that David's reading level was two years behind grade level. I told him about my concerns regarding David's behavior, and although he was receptive, there was no change. I later learned that David did not live with or like his father, and his mother worked long hours and was not always available to work with him. Other students were vocal about their preference of him not being in class. And to be honest, so was I. The other students deserved to learn, and David's behavior was not fair to them. Every day with David felt like we lived the same day again without either of us learning how to make things better. I felt I was doing everything right until David would push things too far. He would yet again insult another student, I would find myself yelling to interrupt it, and then we would be standing, facing one another, as I would tell him he had to leave. David was constantly in detention and was suspended several times for his behavior.

We sometimes fail to pause and consider how students' behaviors affect us, both in how we feel and how we respond. Take a moment to consider the following questions.

- How do you feel when students are resistant, defiant, or disruptive?

- How often are your most difficult relationships with students who do not perform well academically? What might that mean?

- What are some of the ways you have responded? What has felt constructive and what has felt less successful?

Let us consider not only the disrupters. There are students who do not give us trouble, but who we do not really know.

Sometimes we choose to protect our egos in experiences like these by dismissing a particular student as a troublemaker. And although we might think our teaching would be easier or our classroom would run more smoothly if certain students were not in our classroom, perhaps that student is telling us something important about the teacher we need to be.

As Carla Shalaby asks in her brilliant work *Troublemakers:*

Lessons in Freedom from Young Children at School (2017), are these students the canaries in the coal mine, letting us know that our classroom and behaviors do not make all students feel as safe and supported as they could be?

And let us consider not only the disrupters. There are students who do not give us trouble, but who we do not really know, as Jaleel shows in his classroom reflection.

From Jaleel's Classroom

No Participation, But No Complaints

From day one in my classroom, Kionna had a certain maturity about her that many of her peers did not, but she was rather reserved and often mumbled under her breath rather than speaking out loud. Kionna would rarely raise her hand in class even though more times than not she had the correct answer. She remained distant from peers and adults during the day and did not seem to enjoy the company of other people. Because there were so many students who did want and need my attention, it was easy for me to forget Kionna, and I often found myself surprised to hear her voice after several weeks of silence. Kionna did all her work extraordinarily well, but she refused to work with other students. I tried to form a relationship with Kionna by occasionally asking her questions about things that were not school related, but Kionna rarely gave me responses that were more than one or two words.

To see how Jaleel worked to improve his relationship with Kionna, see Section 3, pages 78–79.

As you think about how similar situations play out in your classroom, consider the students who seem "fine." They are compliant with your expected behaviors, but how well do you know them? Sometimes "easy" becomes "invisible" as we tend to issues that more urgently demand our attention, and we give easy students little opportunity to be known beyond complying with the norms of our classroom. We offer only benign neglect; the student is doing well enough under existing conditions, so need we do more?

Self-Assess Your Relationship with Your Students

Are our teacher-student relationships strong enough? Consider the following questions in Figure 1.1. Then take a moment to reflect on students from your current class list. Put a check by each student's name when the answer to the question is yes.

FIGURE 1.1 *Questions for Examining Your Student Relationships*

- Do I greet the student by name each day?
- Do we talk about nonacademic as well as academic topics that interest the student?
- Does the student know I care? Would the student describe our relationship as positive?
- When the student has difficulty, do they know I will work to help?
- Do the student and I laugh together?
- Does the student know who I am beyond the classroom?
- Do I know who the student is beyond the classroom?
- Does the student have evidence to track their progress in my class?
- Does the student think I believe they are smart?

We know that part of the problem with the student examples we shared was that we could not answer yes to most of these questions for those students. (There are also students for whom we can answer yes to most of these questions, but with whom we still have difficulty. We will get to strategies for that later, but this reflective activity is step one.)

Look at the students about whom you answered yes to three or fewer questions. Choose one student to focus on. Take a brief moment to identify and describe what the challenges are in your relationship as Tanya and Jaleel have done in this section. There is no shame in difficulty. It is what we do in response to difficulty that matters. We want you to return to this challenging relationship after reading Section 3 and identify some new strategies to try.

Thanks for taking the time to reflect. This is an essential practice to relationship-building in the classroom. We cannot always be our best selves in the present moment. Reflection helps us prepare for a better future with students. In light of that, let us read what the research tells us about teacher-student relationships to find some answers to our difficulty.

SECTION **2**

WHY NOT?

*Learning Requires
a Relationship*

TYRONE C. HOWARD

Know Your Students Well

// "No significant learning can occur without a significant relationship."

So stated noted student psychiatrist James Comer over thirty years ago (1980, 1993) and subsequent research supports this; students who believe they are cared for by their teachers are not only more engaged (Teven and McCroskey 1997) but achieve higher academic performance (Miller 2008).

And yet . . .

Too many students pass through school feeling unknown, uncared for, unsupported, and disengaged. These students come to believe that school is not a place for them, and if they do not belong there, where do they belong? By and large, this does not happen because today's teachers are an uncaring lot. We know teachers are not given enough clarity, modeling, and accountability to build positive relationships with students. Instead they are given too many scripts that allow them to disengage (Shalaby 2017). (Some of these scripts for disengagement we shared in Section 1.)

Too many students pass through school feeling unknown, uncared for, unsupported, and disengaged.

The idea that learning is built from and through relationships did not originate with Comer. It has always been a part of who we are. What is new is the research that proves how difficult it is to learn without a positive relationship, particularly for students who are disadvantaged by trauma and entrenched structural inequities.

In his book *Social: Why Our Brains Are Wired to Connect*, psychologist and neuroscientist Matthew Lieberman (2013) explains that the human brain's primary purpose is to build relationships between people. According to the work of anthropologist Robin Dunbar (2014), the brain's size reflects the size of its desired social group. The human brain is the largest of all animals in proportion to our body. In other words, we are built to be part of a community of relationships. Our minds have evolved to crave social bonding and to experience social rejection/isolation as intensely as physical pain. (Lieberman's work suggests that this neurological similarity means that pain killers can be effective for social pain as well as physical pain.) Meaning, when students do not have strong social connections in school, where they spend six to seven hours a day, they suffer intensely.

When students do not have strong social connections in school, where they spend six to seven hours a day, they suffer intensely.

We know that in American society right now, the rate of depression is increasing overall, especially among youth (Weinberger et al. 2017). Likewise, the rate of materialism has grown, with 81 percent of college students prioritizing financial success over goals like helping others (Smith 2013). That is not a critique of today's youth but of the climate we have created. Too many of our public conversations deny our essential nature and needs as humans. For example, in conversations about education, we talk about "success" and "college and career readiness" but we do so outside of the context of human relationships. Instead of denying our essential needs, Lieberman suggests a three-pronged relationship-building approach for teachers and schools. (See Figure 2.1.)

We need to contextualize learning beyond college and career success and offer students purpose based on human relationships. For this kind of curriculum planning, see Section 3, pages 52–58, 70–72, and 82–85.

FIGURE 2.1 *How Teachers and Schools Should Support Students' Needs for Connection*

1. Promote connectedness among students and address social pain (isolation and bullying).

2. Teach with social minds as context. Understand that the human brain encodes information socially —which means that we learn things better if they are about people and relationships rather than about abstract facts.

   For specific strategies for each of Lieberman's principles, see Section 3.

3. Promote learning together, rather than learning alone. The ability to cognitively and emotionally share thoughts, ideas, and understanding in a collaborative fashion has significant potential for increased comprehension and learning.

The research recognizes that when you engage the whole student's self through meaningful relationships in school, all aspects of the student's identity grow; investing in positive teacher-student relationships not only improves students' academic performance but also decreases conflict and increases independence, closeness, and support. (See Figure 2.2.)

FIGURE 2.2 *Academic Effects of Positive Teacher-Student Relationships*

- Students adjust better to school, improve social skills and development, succeed academically, and show resilience (Battistich, Schaps, and Wilson 2004; Birch and Ladd 1997; Curby et al. 2009; Ewing and Taylor 2009; Hamre and Pianta 2001; Rudasill et al. 2006).

- Students are less likely to avoid school, appear more self-directed, and are more cooperative and engaged in learning (Birch and Ladd 1997; Decker, Dona, and Christenson 2007; Klem and Connell 2004).

More Time with Students Improves Relationships and Achievement

We know that the teacher-student relationship is a necessary investment for learning. Research also points to the ways school structures can get in the way of that relationship. Recently, economist Roland Fryer (2018) studied the effectiveness of platooning (when teachers specialize in a particular subject such as English or math and students switch teachers for each class) versus teachers staying with the same students all day. Frequent transitioning between classes may prevent teachers from having full information on a student's "state of the world" for that particular day (621). Fryer discovered that elementary students taught by specialists (platooning) did worse on reading and math scores than students taught by a single teacher. Moreover, he found suspensions and absences were also higher in schools that tried platooning. Students identified as having special needs scored three times lower on high-stakes tests and two times worse on low-stakes tests compared with students who stayed with the same teacher throughout the day. In short, Fryer (2018) contends that the specialization approach used in platooning is similar to the assembly line model for automobiles, but "pupils are not pins, and the production of human capital is far more complex than assembling automobiles" (617). Hill and Jones (2018) further support these conclusions by drawing on rich statewide administrative data. They found small, yet significant, test score gains for students assigned to the same teacher for a second time in a higher grade (looping). It is worth noting that gains were higher for non-white students and for students whose teachers were less effective and experienced. Their findings suggest that there could be potential low-cost gains from "looping" and seem connected to the recent experimental evidence that teacher specialization has negative effects on student achievement, given that this likely decreases student-teacher familiarity.

Teacher specialization has negative effects on student achievement, given that this likely decreases student-teacher familiarity.

We acknowledge that it is not in every teacher's control to shift from a platooning to a same-teacher-all-day model or from having students just one year to a looping model, but the idea that more time with students improves relationships and student outcomes points to devoting more time to getting to know your students.

Communicate with Parents and Caregivers

Relationship-building with families and caregivers is not a "nice to do." It's a necessity. The research is abundantly clear that students do better when teachers and school staff communicate regularly with parents and caregivers. According to Henderson et al. (2007),

- Students whose families are involved in their schooling earn better grades, have higher graduation rates, and are more likely to enroll in postsecondary education.

- When families have a positive attitude toward school, students do, too.

- Students of Color do better when families are involved in schools.

- Middle and high school students whose families remain involved make better transitions, are more likely to engage in rigorous coursework, and are less likely to drop out of school.

That does not mean it is always easy. For home communication to benefit students, educators must work hard to dismantle deficit beliefs about certain parents and caregivers. Many educators make assumptions that some caregivers are not concerned about their students' education (Reynolds, Howard, and Jones 2015). Instead, teachers need to have an asset-based approach to parent and caregiving relationships. We need to recognize that there is no one right way to be a good parent, honor the multiple ways that adults raise students (e.g., grandparents, older siblings, relative caregivers, foster parents), and support their families. For some parents and caregivers from economically disadvantaged backgrounds, the challenge of providing housing and food security can leave little time or energy for anything else; attending school events is just not possible. Some parents and caregivers work two or three jobs to make ends meet, and some parents and caregivers have the added responsibility of caring for

We need to recognize that there is no one right way to be a good parent, honor the multiple ways that adults raise students (e.g., grandparents, older siblings, relative caregivers, foster parents), and support their families.

aging parents, grandparents, and family members. Issues such as transportation and care for younger students can also make attending school events a challenge. Rather than judging caregivers who cannot participate, schools need to be more creative in communicating and establishing teacher-caregiver relationships. School personnel must take responsibility for initiating and maintaining ongoing, valuable, and accessible communication to parents and caregivers.

For specific strategies on communicating with families, see Section 3, pages 68–76.

Foster Positive Peer Relationships

Awareness cannot begin and end with relationships between teachers, their individual students, and the students' families; teachers need to recognize the daily challenges many students encounter with their peers and the positive benefits that come from a sense of belonging. Students' dispositions and their interactions with peers create school climate as much as teachers' interactions with students. Knowing students means understanding the school community students exist in and actively working to make it positive. This is even more critical given the prevalence of bullying in today's schools and its profound effect on students' academic, emotional, and social well-being.

Knowing students means understanding the school community students exist in and actively working to make it positive.

According to the U.S. Department of Health and Human Services (StopBullying.gov):

- 20 percent of students ages 12–18 experienced bullying (2017).

- 15 percent of students ages 12–18 who reported being bullied at school were bullied online or by text (2017).

- About 30 percent of young people admit to bullying others in surveys.

- 70.6 percent of young people said they have seen bullying in their schools.

- 40.6 percent of students reported some type of frequent involvement in bullying.

    - 23.2 percent of students were frequently bullied.

    - 8.0 percent of students frequently bullied others.

    - 9.4 percent of students played both roles frequently.

- Only about 20–30 percent of students who are bullied notify adults about the bullying.

- 70.4 percent of school staff has witnessed bullying.

- 33 percent of LGB students report being bullied on school property in the past year (2017).

- 27.1 percent of LGB students report being cyberbullied in the past year (2017).

Because peer relationships can play such a big role in bullying and its prevention, teachers need to be aware of which students are socially isolated or excluded from peer groups. There is a growing body of evidence about the long-term impacts of this experience, including what we shared earlier about the impact of emotional pain on learning (Eisenberger, Lieberman, and Williams 2003).

Students take on the identity of bully for a variety of reasons: because they are uncomfortable with some aspect of themselves, are demonstrating behavior they have experienced, and/or need guidance on how to gain positive attention. Regardless of the reason, the perpetrator needs the same positive adult relationships and self-esteem building that we want for the victims of bullying. Students also benefit from understanding that there are often more than two roles in a bullying situation: the perpetrator, the victim, and the bystander. According to the U.S. Department of Health and Human Services, "When bystanders intervene, bullying stops within ten seconds 57 percent of the time" (StopBullying. gov). Educators can teach students how to address bullying by helping students understand how damaging it is and by setting expectations and guidelines for students to intervene. This

"When bystanders intervene, bullying stops within ten seconds 57 percent of the time" (U.S. Department of Health and Human Services).

fulfills an essential element of relationship-building: "I care about you. You matter. Your safety matters to me." And when other students see that you, the educator, will stand up for and care for students in need, their relationship with you deepens as well. They understand that this is an inclusive community where everyone deserves to feel safe and welcome.

Teaching and Relationship-Building Must Be Culturally Responsive

What do students see, hear, feel, and do in their daily environments? The answers reveal who our students are, what and who are important in their lives, and should be the basis of our curriculum.

> We need to build positive student-student relationships. For stopping microaggressions, see Section 3, pages 44–49. For creating opportunities for meaningful collaboration, see Section 3, pages 82–83.

Our relationships with students should describe more than our classroom community; it must also describe our curriculum. Students' sociocultural identity—their customs, cultural practices, communication norms, and values—is not a static label, but rather, can be a tool to gather strength and to move beyond limiting realities. Gloria Ladson-Billings describes this as culturally responsive work "that not only addresses student achievement but also helps students to accept and affirm their cultural identity while developing critical perspectives that challenge inequities that schools (and other institutions) perpetuate" (1995). Culturally responsive curriculum can take many shapes and forms. From using students' preferred common vernacular, idioms, and phrases to incorporating content and examples from their social media, music, movie references, and video gaming preferences—the form is specific to the context of the students in your classroom. For example, some students may have a strong orientation toward injustice, and may be more vocal in the classroom when they see or experience injustice, because in their respective home or community, unfairness and injustice are not accepted. So, it is important to have curriculum that addresses these students'

> *What do students see, hear, feel, and do in their daily environments? The answers reveal who our students are, what and who are important in their lives, and should be the basis of our curriculum.*

expectation or core cultural value of speaking up about injustice even if you are not the person involved. It is up to teachers to take an anthropological approach to recognize core aspects of students' lives, such as:

- home, life, community context;
- learning preferences;
- communication modalities;
- content consumed (current events, interests, and media);
- core values.

By understanding the larger culture, our identities within existing systems of oppression, and the cultures of our students, we can recreate a better world in our classrooms. As Geneva Gay explains, our pedagogy can be built around these ideas "to and through the strengths of these students" (2018, 36). When teachers take on the work of culturally responsive teaching, they commit to ensuring that marginalized students not only can, but will improve their school achievement (Gay 2018, 69). One important aspect of a culturally responsive approach to teaching is that school curriculum, instruction,

> Teacher behaviors that are intended to be culturally responsive can cross the line to cultural appropriation. In short, a teacher should not adopt behaviors from a culture that is not their own. For more specific guidelines, see Section 3, page 51.

and learning are tied to students' experiences, realities, identities, histories, and in many ways their expertise. High performance is an expectation and consequently the norm. (For more on culturally responsive teaching, see *No More Culturally Irrelevant Teaching* [Souto-Manning et al. 2018].)

An extension of culturally responsive teaching is culturally sustaining pedagogy (Paris and Alim 2017), which challenges teachers to go beyond mere acknowledgment, acceptance, or tolerance of students' cultural identities and to move instead toward explicitly supporting aspects of their languages, literacies, and cultural traditions. Culturally sustaining pedagogy encourages teachers to understand and employ the term *culture* in a broader sense, incorporating popular, youth, and local culture alongside ethnicity. Examples of culturally sustaining practices include encouraging students' use of culturally familiar languages in the classroom; these practices could also include ethnic studies content that takes a more critical approach to history, bringing issues of oppression, domination, and colonialism front and center. Culturally sustaining pedagogy could also prioritize student agency by encouraging students to make their lives, experiences, language, and literacies a frequent starting point for understanding new concepts, issues, and content in the curriculum.

Race Matters

Race has been and remains one of the more undertheorized and misunderstood concepts in schools and society (Howard 2020). And race matters. Racial literacy, which education scholar Howard Stevenson (2014) defines as "the ability to read and recast, or reduce and resolve, racially stressful encounters during face-to-face interactions," can go a long way toward establishing and maintaining relationships with racially diverse students. Today's student population is racially and ethnically far more diverse than today's teaching population:

Today's student population is racially and ethnically far more diverse than today's teaching population.

- Students of Color make up more than 50 percent of the nation's student population.

- About 80 percent of classroom teachers are white, a decrease from 82 percent in 2012.

- Teachers of Color are grossly underrepresented in the United States, making up only 18 percent of all classroom teachers:

  - Approximately 9 percent of teachers are Latinx, up from 8 percent previously.

  - Seven percent of teachers are African American (the same since 2012).

  - Two percent are Asian American (the same since 2012).

(The U.S. Department of Education 2016; National Center for Educational Statistics 2017).

Some disturbing data tell us that white teachers are more likely to underestimate the abilities and academic potential of Students of Color, tend to have lower expectations for them, and often express less connectedness with them (Tenenbaum and Ruck 2007). This same research also shows that Teachers of Color tend to have higher expectations for all students, are more culturally responsive with their content, and are often mentioned by students of all racial backgrounds as their preferred teachers. More recently, a study revealed that students of all races prefer Teachers of Color because of the levels of care, support, and sensitivity that they provide compared with their white counterparts (Cherng and Halpin 2016).

In a study on teacher-student racial match, Downer et al. (2016) and his colleagues found that young Latinx students who were not proficient in English were more likely to develop higher early literacy skills when their teachers were also Latinx. The study also found that Black teachers rated Black students' language and literacy skills higher upon school entry in the fall than white teachers did but tended to report fewer gains in those skills at the end of the year, leading researchers to hypothesize that Black teachers have higher standards for Black students. Downer suggested that white teachers' lower expectations seemed to be due to lack of culturally responsive tools to support Black students or due to implicit bias wherein they had lower expectations for Black students.

Teachers of Color tend to have higher expectations for all students, are more culturally responsive with their content, and are often mentioned by students of all racial backgrounds as their preferred teachers.

The research on same-race teachers and students reveals important insight into attitudes, beliefs, and expectations that Teachers of Color tend to have for Students of Color. Issues of race, racism, and cultural understanding all speak to the utility of having more Teachers of Color in schools for all students. However, we want to be clear that teacher-student race matching alone does not guarantee student success or the ability to formulate healthy teacher-student relationships. Teachers who incorporate asset-based teaching practices, have an awareness of the sociopolitical context of students'

For strategies on repairing broken academic faith, see Section 3, pages 79–80.

realities, and have sound racial literacy and cultural competence can also cultivate relationships with students even if they are not of the same racial background as their students.

Build and Protect Students' Self-Esteem

The most foundational asset-based teaching practice is to build students' self-esteem. Many students enter classrooms full of uncertainty, insecurity, and doubt about who they are, where they fit in, and who they are striving to become. They withdraw, concealing their fear, pain, and suffering, or may display aggression, unless they feel safe. Teachers can invite students to be their full selves in the classroom by creating a positive classroom community, one that boosts rather than diminishes students' self-esteem. First, words matter—both what we say and what others say in our school community. Our words should encourage students' efforts and convey an honest and persistent belief in students' ability to be successful. Simple acts are part of the work, like acknowledging students' presence in a classroom with a smile or saying, "It is good to see you today. I am glad that you are here." Management professor Mary Rowe (2008) describes these as microaffirmations, frequent, subtle, yet explicit acts of kindness, inclusion, care, or small acknowledgments of a person's value, presence, efforts, and accomplishments. Micro-affirmations can go a long way in communicating to students that:

For more information on how to give students micro-affirmations, see Section 3, pages 42–44.

- You are important.
- I see you.
- I value you.
- I am here to support you.
- You are cared for.
- You are safe here.

Micro-affirmations are important for all students but can have added value for Students of Color who may be dealing with racial discrimination or exclusion in the classroom or school

(Pérez Huber and Solórzano 2015). Educational scholar Lindsay Pérez Huber (2018) states that:

> Racial micro-affirmations are a response to systemic everyday racism, such as racial microaggressions, in that they provide commonplace strategies to resist the subjection of Communities of Color . . . they are (1) verbal and/or non-verbal affirmations, (2) layered affirmations based on race, and (3) cumulative affirmation that have positive psychological and physiological effects." (2)

Knowing and accurately pronouncing names is a form of micro-affirmation (Kohli and Solórzano 2012), as is recognizing and respecting home languages. Seeking to build on students' primary language recognizes that what they already know has value; seeking to replace students' primary language by insisting "English-only in this classroom" devalues students' identity and makes the classroom an unsafe space.

H. Richard Milner (2010) has further helped teachers focus on building students' self-esteem by replacing the deficit language of "achievement gaps," which blames Students of Color and their families for academic struggle, with "opportunity gaps," which invites educators to rethink their practices. This work is not merely a change in vocabulary but focuses on negating five specific areas of deficit thinking in education. (See Figure 2.3.)

FIGURE 2.3 *How Teachers Must Welcome All Students*

1. Reject color blindness.
2. Understand and navigate cultural conflicts.
3. Dismantle the myth of meritocracy.
4. Eradicate low expectation and deficit mindsets.
5. Reject context-neutral mindsets.

Reject Color Blindness

Given the growing divide between the racial identities of today's teacher population and today's student population, an important aspect of relationship-building is for teachers to support students, particularly those from non-white backgrounds, in developing a healthy racial awareness. This means acknowledging students' racial identities and having a sociopolitical and historical awareness of the role that race and racism have played and continue to play in our society. This is not possible if teachers aim to be color blind. When teachers say they do not see race, they tell students their lives are not of significance. They miss an opportunity to develop racial awareness and connect to students' racial realities—their own as well as their students'.

When teachers say they do not see race, they tell students their lives are not of significance.

Understand and Navigate Cultural Conflict

Milner maintains that "when teachers operate from their own cultural ways of knowing the learning milieu can be foreign to students whose cultural experiences are different and inconsistent with teachers' experiences" (2015, 24). Language, examples, idioms, phrases, forms of communication, interests, and hobbies—how much classroom dialogue privileges teachers' ways of knowing over students? A teacher's job is not to teach students how to be like them but how to participate in the world, and so multiple ways of knowing the world must be present in the classroom with none privileged over others. Culturally responsive and culturally sustaining pedagogies create space for students' ways of knowing. Teachers can navigate potential conflicts by expressing cultural humility; by listening and learning about students' ways of knowing, doing, thinking, and expressing; and by explicitly stating to students that they may be unfamiliar with some of the students' personal, social and linguistic capital.

For ways to recognize students' and families' ways of knowing, see Section 3, pages 50–56 and pages 68–72.

Because today's schools reflect a growing ethnic, linguistic, cultural, and racial diversity due to immigration, teachers must embrace the cultural, geographical, and linguistic differences in their classrooms:

- With the largest number of immigrants in the world, forty-five million people in the United States are foreign born (Pew Research Center 2015). The greatest number of immigrants in the United States right now are from Asia, Latin America, and Africa.

- Approximately 25 percent of students under the age of eighteen or a total of almost nineteen million students have an immigrant parent (Suárez-Orozco and Michikyan 2016).

- There are more than 350 languages spoken in the United States, and over half of them by immigrants (U.S. Census Bureau 2015). In the United States, there are seven non-English languages with more than one million speakers:

    - Spanish (38.4 million)

    - Chinese (3 million)

    - Tagalog (1.6 million)

    - Vietnamese (1.4 million)

    - French (1.3 million)

    - Korean (1.1 million)

    - Arabic (1.1 million).

Understanding the important role that language has in identity, family, history, culture, and struggle is vital for relationship-building. Many language learners come to school full of anxiety, fear, uncertainty, and doubt about their ability to be successful in school (Suárez-Orozco 2018). Educators who acknowledge and affirm students' primary language, if it is not English, let students understand that they are safe and secure in their classrooms and that students' ways of knowing, communicating, and processing are important and valued.

Dismantle the Myth of Meritocracy

The American education system was built on a myth of meritocracy that sorts "worthy" students from the "unworthy." This unjust system perpetuates itself by explaining success or failure based on individual merit, effort, and hard work. Such a belief renders oppression, exclusion, and discrimination as insignificant. Yet in actuality, those who end up "worthy" in this system are disproportionately white and economically privileged. Teachers must understand the history of struggle and prejudice against marginalized groups (e.g., People of Color, women, LGBTQIA+, and immigrants) and make sure issues such as privilege, opportunity, advantage, and benefits are thoroughly understood and taught to students.

> *Teachers cannot take a socially, economically, and politically unconscious approach to where they work and the conditions that students encounter daily outside of school.*

Eradicate Low Expectations and Deficit Mindsets

Teachers' beliefs and expectations can have a profound influence on students' ability to learn. It has been noted for decades that students can often live up to or down to the expectations teachers have for them (Rist 1970; de Boer et al. 2018). Teachers must be clear that they do not think less of certain students because of their language, socioeconomic status, race, or home life circumstances. Teachers must also fight the tendency to "feel sorry" or lower their standards for students because of their personal or family situation. Holding all students to high, age-appropriate expectations is an absolute must for all educators.

Reject Context-Neutral Mindsets

Milner (2010) states that "context neutral mindsets do not allow educators to recognize the realities embedded in a particular place, such as a school in a particular community" (37). Not all schools operate in the same space and place; diversity and opportunity are not consistent in every school: poverty, gentrification, and racial landscape matter. Teachers cannot take a socially, economically, and politically unconscious approach to where they work and the conditions that students encounter daily outside of school.

Refrain from Judgment

Easier said than done, but we are not pretending teachers do not make judgments, because we all do. Rather, we are asking teachers to be self-aware enough to monitor for them so that they can prevent them from negatively affecting students. Many young people want to share their lives with adults but are afraid of our judgment, especially if they know their lives and decision-making do not fit traditional expectations. To feel safe, students need us to listen without judgment. Even if the circumstances require a future action from us, such as mandatory reporting, in the moment of sharing, we need to be calm and steady for the student. Although that is hard to do at times, it is always necessary. Most people do not feel listened to enough, and that is especially true for young people. If we want students to have positive understanding about their lives, we need to be a supportive audience as they make sense of it for themselves. Of course, ideally, we have the kind of teacher-student relationship where the student wants to hear what we think, but listen first, then ask the student if they want to hear our thoughts. Figure 2.4 presents some teaching guidelines based on a range of studies.

To feel safe, students need us to listen without judgment.

FIGURE 2.4 *Four Steps to Help Teachers Refrain from Judgment*

---

1. Practice active listening.

Lean forward and be physically and emotionally present when talking with a student. Focus on the student and on what they are trying to communicate. Repeat what the student says to make sure you understand the thought, question, or comment. Follow up with questions that show your interest and that can help the student draw their own conclusions.

2. Recognize and validate every student experience.

This does not mean agreeing with the student's interpretation of the experience or the student's reaction to the experience. This means making clear to the student that you understand the challenge of the experience they are expressing, and that you are here to help them consider productive ways of dealing with it. It is also important to offer appropriate verbal, written, and body language cues that demonstrate you are interested and care about what the student is sharing.

3. Affirm student feelings.

Validate students' feeling through statements such as "I appreciate that this is frustrating," "I can see why this would upset you," "I see that you are excited by this opportunity," or "I understand that you are disappointed." Validate feelings while steering students toward developing productive and multiple perspectives on the same situation to build empathy.

4. Help students optimally process academic experiences.

Ask students questions that will help them reflect on their behaviors in class and their academic experiences, as well as help them to explore their thinking, decisions, feelings, reactions, and options. Asking questions such as "What led to that decision?," "Tell me why you think this happened?," and "What will you do differently next time?" These questions can help students process their emotions and experiences in a way that will help them plan productively for the future and grow as students.

Perspective taking, or the ability to adopt or imagine another person's psychological point of view (Davis 1994), is a research-proven technique to refrain from judgment by fostering empathy. There is compelling research evidence of other "helping professions" (such as nursing, social work, medicine, and counseling) whose application of empathy improves the outcomes of those we are trying to help. In education, empathy has been theorized to improve the quality of teachers' reaction or response to the needs of diverse students, but too little empirical research exists that operationalizes the application of empathy in teaching. One of the more impressive bodies of research by education professor Chezare Warren (2015, 2018) identifies the "empathy gap" experienced by many Students of Color in schools. He describes this as the "disparity in perception between those on the receiving end of one's help and the helper" (573). Empathy requires educators to see the world through the eyes of marginalized students and to understand how the world has seen them. And yet how many teachers understand the systems of oppression that have kept Students of Color from succeeding? Although many early career educators say they believe in fairness, perspective taking, and equity in their interactions with students, their actions often contradict their stated beliefs (Warren 2015, 2018). Specifically, in his research Warren identified that teachers' description of their empathic beliefs was disproven by how they interacted with Black male students, and that many of their interactions with students did not reflect empathy or perspective taking. Often, teachers were reluctant to show the vulnerability necessary for relationship-building, explaining that they were not "touchy feely" or "a hugger" and were averse to demonstrating too much emotion toward their Black male students (185). Of course, coldness and disdain are not the only unproductive teacher behaviors in relationships. Some teachers mistake sympathy for empathy (Howard 2020). They are not the same. When educators feel sorry for students, that is not equity, that is pity. Educators' pity is a negative judgment that lowers expectations and allows Students of Color to fail.

> *Empathy requires educators to see the world through the eyes of marginalized students and to understand how the world has seen them.*

Expect Indifference and Defiance

Educators must understand that their interactions with students are informed by the sum of all previous interactions (good and bad) that students have had with adults, including previous teachers. Students who rebuff teachers' efforts to connect are only communicating that life has given them reason not to trust adults. Anger, mistrust, and detachment can be a student's reasonable response to mistreatment. A teacher's necessary response is to keep showing up in positive ways to earn the student's trust. Sometimes, a student's initial behavior is only intended to test whether the adult will give up on them or not. Of course, some behaviors are normal social development phases for students, such as testing limits, resistance, and silence. Teachers need to avoid misreading these phases as defiance (Shalaby 2017). This understanding is an equity issue as Students of Color, in particular, are often mislabeled for being disrespectful and willfully defiant in schools.

Students who rebuff teachers' efforts to connect are only communicating that life has given them reason not to trust adults.

Resilience Grows Through Relationships

Too many schools today operate by the misguided belief that students need to just put forth greater effort, tenacity, and perseverance, or what Angela Duckworth (2016) refers to as "grit." Because of the popularity of this damaging belief, it is essential to tell the story of the research to properly debunk it. Duckworth inferred her conclusion from a survey of high performers, but she herself admits that her questions were problematic and that her data only answered the question of whether high performers are conscientious (Barshay 2019). What Duckworth did not do is telling. She did not identify what teachers do to foster students' achievement. As Jal Mehta explains, "Most people do not persevere at things because they are good at persevering, they persevere because they find things that are worth investing in. The implication for schools is that they should spend less time trying to boost students' grit, and more time trying to think about how their offerings could help students develop purpose and passion" (2015).

It is not just that the research behind grit is flawed but that the assumption behind grit is dangerous and deficit-laden. Grit assumes students are not already putting forth maximum effort under incredibly difficult circumstances. Duckworth's framing talks about the talent, skill, and effort that lead to grit but admits "my theory doesn't address outside factors" (42). Yet outside factors matter. Complex trauma compromises students' ability to concentrate on learning. Over 2.5 million students experience homelessness every year (The National Center on Family Homelessness). How can a student think about homework, when they do not know where they will sleep at night? It is important too to acknowledge that grit can be domain specific. The student who does not demonstrate grit for an algebra problem may show uncanny grit when it comes to figuring out how to feed, protect, and nurture younger siblings in the absence of adults.

Resilience grows through relationships, not through will alone. Poverty, homelessness, abuse, neglect, discrimination, racial microaggressions, gender bias, homophobia, underfunded schools, inexperienced teachers, and other "outside factors" explain a lot when it comes to how well students learn. We would argue that students who stand in the face of these "outside factors" with teachers who have lowered expectations, inadequate schooling conditions, and test-obsessed classrooms demonstrate grit every day in just showing up for school. Education scholar Bettina Love (2019) elaborates further on the problems when she says:

> *Resilience grows through relationships, not through will alone.*

> Measuring students' grit and zest, and reminding them that there are "no excuses" sounds like an easy fix for oppression, but telling dark students that they need to pull themselves up by their bootstraps and achieve on their own merit is not a new approach; it is short-sighted and, in actuality, racist thinking. (76)

We completely reject the idea that students fail to succeed because of a lack of grit. Of course, mindset, hard work, perseverance, and problem-solving affect goal achievement, but students need teachers who know them and who understand the larger systems of oppression in society. Authentic relationship-building recognizes the grit that is already inherent in young people and their caregivers rather than only acknowledging what is shown in a traditional school context. Good teachers honor the challenging day-to-day realities that many students endure to seek and secure the safety, health, security, and well-being of themselves and others. Good teachers show students that they manifest grit every day in their effort to maintain their humanity, hold on to their sanity, and claim their right to learn, often in the face of extreme adversity.

Authentic Relationship-Building Is Based on Reciprocity

The work around relationships is paradoxical. So much of the work is simple. Being caring, kind, considerate, empathetic, aware, and a good listener are not complicated actions. Starting with these behaviors and mindsets is more than enough to put teachers on the right track of student-teacher relationships. However, relationship-building is also culturally mediated, which means that it does not look the same for all students. When we expect all students to show respect and attention in the same ways, for example, then we are showing them disrespectful attention; we are seeing only one way of being, and so, negating others. As the nation's schools become more diverse, the convergence of culture, identity, race, language, personality, lived experiences, and personal preferences requires teachers' humility, flexibility, reflection, and resourcefulness to build and sustain positive student relationships. The resources and research offered in this section do not seek to simplify the intricacies of this work. At times, students may resent or not want our efforts to connect with them. Our ongoing work is to keep showing up for students so that we are available when they are ready to connect.

We also invite teachers and researchers to take on the needed work of envisioning what culturally responsive and culturally sustaining relationships look like across schools. There is much to be gained from understanding how many teachers, administrators, and staff are currently doing this work, and doing it well. We hope that the principles provided in this section can be helpful in more meaningful, equity-focused teacher-student relationships. Authentic relationship-building is based on reciprocity. In the next section, Tanya and Jaleel will offer specific examples of these principles in practice.

SECTION **3**

BUT **THAT**

*Teaching From
and Through Your
Relationships
with Students*

JALEEL R. HOWARD, TANYA MILNER-McCALL, TYRONE C. HOWARD

As soon as you walk into a school, you can sense the general quality of the relationships in that space. Do people pass by one another without eye contact or are students excited to see and speak with their teachers? Do adults greet students by name? Do students and teachers talk to one another affectionately? These brief interactions accumulate to define a relationship and those relationships define the culture of a school.

There is no one way to make every relationship positive and trusting. Relationship-building, like learning, is contextual. In this section you will find a collection of strategies that, with modification based on context, can be used to build and maintain relationships with your students. For most of us, there may be times when we need to temporarily walk away from a situation because we are overwhelmed and want to avoid saying or doing the wrong thing. That is normal. This work is never done perfectly. We all misstep. The only essential practice is holding ourselves accountable to working toward positive relationships with *all* students in our care.

> *The only essential practice is holding ourselves accountable to working toward positive relationships with* all *students in our care.*

As Tyrone explained in Section 2, a negative relationship between teacher and student diminishes the learning potential of that student. In the examples in this section, we hope you also find evidence that positive teacher-student relationships do not just transform student learning, but also bring great joy to the teacher. Each day invites us to create the kind of positive connection that could change a student's life.

39

Students' Desire to Be Known

As the examples we shared in Section 1 showed, some relationships begin in difficulty: "You do not know me!" "I hate you!" "Leave me alone!" In disgust and anger, students speak back, either to the adult who is not meeting their needs or to a history of bad treatment. Sometimes students express themselves wordlessly: pulling the string of their hoodie tight to hide part of their face, placing their head down on their desk, skipping school, or giving an indifferent shrug in response to another missed assignment. Students' disengagement is often a defensive response to feeling misunderstood, invisible, or not valued.

Students' disengagement is often a defensive response to feeling misunderstood, invisible, or not valued.

These types of responses can make us feel defensive, too. Receiving that indifference and disdain can make us question our ability to teach. The unacknowledged weight of challenging relationships can make us feel so unseen, unknown, and unvalued that we ignore or dismiss students and lean into our position as an adult with power, until both teacher and student have a script of avoiding each other as human beings. That circle of frustration can feel so tight that any other pattern seems impossible. Regardless of how it feels, it is not impossible, but it does require choosing vulnerability. Being vulnerable requires leaving ourselves open to judgment and criticism. Openness is necessary for connection and transformation; avoiding vulnerability is a form of self-denial. As Brené Brown says, "To feel is to be vulnerable. Believing that vulnerability is weakness is believing that feeling is weakness. And, like it or not, we are emotional beings" (42). So, we choose to reach out to students who may reject us, and we choose to try again if they do reject us, and, most importantly, we never reject them. For school to be a haven for our students, they must have positive relationships with us. Teaching requires that of us. Anything less cheats our students and compromises our collective future.

In small and large ways, we can try new beginnings with students at any time in the school year. Every school year is the possibility for better relationships; every class is the possibility for better relationships; every interaction is the possibility for something better. One of the key ways we have found to improve relationships is to put multiple strategies into action at once. Some will succeed more than others, and it is essential that we find some success because every relationship will face a challenge (as our relationships with families and friends can attest).

We suggest you read through these pages and pick three to five possibilities to focus on.

Every school year is the possibility for better relationships; every class is the possibility for better relationships; every interaction is the possibility for something better.

Language That Builds and Protects Self-Esteem

Our language choices can communicate the opposite of intentions, particularly when we are in challenging situations with students. As Peter Johnston (2004) demonstrates in *Choice Words*, how we talk to students communicates how we view the relationship. (See Figure 3.1.)

FIGURE 3.1 *Implications of Different Teacher Responses to Social Transgression*

Teacher Comment	"That group, get back to work or you will be staying in at lunch."	"When you are loud like that, it interferes with the other discussion groups and I feel frustrated."	"This is not like you. What is the problem you have encountered? OK, how can you solve it?"
Question Answered by Comment			
What are we doing here?	Laboring	Living in cooperation	Living collaboratively
How do we relate to one another?	Authoritarian control	Respectful with equal rights	Working out our problems
How do we relate to what we are studying?	Doing it only under duress	[No implication]	[No implication]

From *Choice Words: How Our Language Affects Children's Learning* by Peter Johnston. Copyright © 2003 by Peter Johnston. Reprinted with permission from Stenhouse Publishers. www.stenhouse.com

The language we use does not just describe our existing relationship, but affects how students respond to us, both academically and socially. Language is an action that builds identity and describes how we feel about each other. We can communicate in ways that break down students and contribute to their feelings of inadequacy or in ways that uplift, affirm their intellect and ways of knowing, and inspire their curiosity. Attending to our language is not always easy. We want to avoid statements that expect only compliance and that communicate students need to be controlled. For many of us, most of the time, we may make comments without thinking about the consequences, and instead follow the thread of our emotions. If we believe that students should be able to control what they say and do, then we should hold ourselves to the same, if not a higher, standard. When we use language that is forceful or hierarchical and limits student response, we represent school as an institution of compliance, one that refuses to recognize students as individuals. When we use language that is positive, invitational, and expansive, then we are students' allies in navigating complicated realities.

Language is not just about which words we choose but how we deliver them.

Language is not just about which words we choose but how we deliver them. We have observed many teachers who feel under such pressure that their voices have a tight, disembodied delivery, as if they are being squeezed by a giant fist. Students sense their teachers' anxiety, which can cause them to feel uneasy, disdainful, or angry, and that in turn prevents them from engaging fully.

For research on micro-affirmations, see Section 2, pages 24–25.

Other times, we say the right words but displace our negative emotions through the delivery, using sarcasm or turning away from students. Education professor Daniel Solórzano has discussed the salience and persistence of racial microaggressions and how they can have an impact on Students of Color academically, socially, and emotionally. (For more details, see Pérez Huber and Solórzano's 2015 *Race Ethnicity and Education* article, "Racial Microaggression as a Tool for Critical Race Research," or their 2015 *Latino Policy & Issues Brief* article, "Microaggressions: What They Are, What They Are Not, and Why They Matter.") Education scholar Lindsay Pérez Huber (2018) talks about the pertinence of using language to dismantle microaggressions, and how to uplift and protect Students of Color, who must frequently ward off racial offenses from school personnel, by using microaffirmations (kind words and affirming messages that convey to students that they matter). Simple statements matter like:

- I am so glad to see you today. We missed you yesterday.
- Thank you for your participation in class today.
- Your brilliance is contagious.

Our praise needs to be sincere and not said reflexively, the way "good job" sometimes is in classrooms. The reality of teaching and learning is that our language is powerful and carries significant weight. Our words can uplift and affirm our students, or they can harm and cut down students. We need to be mindful of both realities. We wish we did not have so many examples of times we have made these mistakes, but catching ourselves in them is the only way we have gotten better.

Figure 3.2 will help you increase your awareness of how you communicate with students.

FIGURE 3.2 *Be More Metacognitive About Your Student Communication*

1. **Make a video recording of a classroom period.** Make certain you have student and caregiver permission to do this beforehand and explain that the purpose is to make you a better teacher. Then watch it on your own or with a close colleague.

   - What language choices did you make that shut students down? How could you have communicated differently?
   - What language choices created space for students to make positive choices?
   - What evidence could you see of each student's emotional, behavioral, and cognitive engagement?
   - Does your body language show that you are interested in what every student has to say? Do you ever seem like you are judging, showing disdain, or frustration?
   - Do you provide more recognition and affirmation to certain students?

2. **Rehearse.** Practice responding to a challenging behavior in a mirror. Consider writing out the words first. Pay close attention to your facial expression. This is something that I (Tanya) have to do often because I sometimes show my students a judging face when I want to show is my supportive teacher face. I have had enough students comment on that stern face that I try to self-monitor for it. I do not want my students to feel judged.

3. **Invite a colleague into your classroom.** If there is a colleague you trust, especially if they are someone who is also thinking about classroom communication, ask them if they will observe you. Before they arrive, set up the visit by choosing a lens through which they may observe (facial expressions, students you tend to call on, students you tend not to call on, responses to student comments, ratio of teacher talk to student talk, etc.) After the visit, set up a time for your colleague to share what they observed. If possible, you might also want to visit their classroom.

Address Microaggressions

Our relationships with students are not just defined by our communication to them but in how we respond to what we observe.

> *Our relationships with students are not just defined by our communication to them but in how we respond to what we observe.*

For research on the impact of bullying, see Section 2, pages 18–20.

Every day, students are exposed to what the late psychiatrist Chester M. Pierce (1969, 1970) called microaggressions, "the verbal, nonverbal, and environmental slights, snubs, or insults, whether intentional or unintentional, that communicate hostile, derogatory, or negative messages to target persons based solely upon their marginalized group membership" (UCLA Diversity and Faculty Development 2014). Microaggressions from peers and staff can be all the evidence a student needs to know school is not for them. See Figure 3.3 for examples of microaggressions. As part of community-building in the beginning of the year, from kindergarten through high school, we define and identify microaggressions so that through awareness and dialogue, we can diminish their occurrence and impact.

FIGURE 3.3 *How to Recognize Microaggressions*

THEMES	MICROAGGRESSION EXAMPLES	UNDERLYING MESSAGE
Alien in One's Own Land Someone who is being perceived as a perpetual foreigner or being an alien in one's own country	▶ Saying to a Latinx- or Asian-American, "So where are you *really* from?" or "You speak really good English" ▶ Continuing to mispro-nounce the names of students after students have corrected the person; not willing to listen closely and learn the pronunciation of an unfamiliar-based name	▶ You're not really an American. You don't really belong here.
Assuming Inherent Abilities or Qualities Making assumptions about a group's intellectual ability, competencies and capabilities; asking someone to speak for their entire race or other social group	▶ Complimenting non-white students on their use of "good English" or being "articulate" ▶ Saying, "You are a credit to your race." ▶ Saying to an Asian student, "You must be good in math, can you help her with this problem?" ▶ Asking people with hidden disabilities to identify themselves in class	▶ You're not as intelligent or you are unusually intelligent. ▶ You must be good or you must not be good at this activity based on your marginalized group status.

THEMES	MICROAGGRESSION EXAMPLES	UNDERLYING MESSAGE
Color Blindness Statements that indicate that a white person does not want to or need to acknowledge race	▶ Saying, "There is only one race, the human race." ▶ Saying, "America is a melting pot." ▶ Saying, "We are all the same so we don't need to talk about our differences."	▶ Denies the experiences of students by questioning the credibility/validity of their stories ▶ Assimilate to the dominant culture. ▶ Denies the role that race plays in societal inequities
Criminality Statements that assume certain groups are dangerous or criminal	▶ Something goes missing and a teacher assumes a Black student stole it ▶ Not wanting one's child to be taught by gays or lesbians ▶ A white student participates in class without being called on and is called "assertive"; a Black boy does the same and is called "aggressive"; Black boys are kept closer to a teacher's desk so that they can be "watched" ▶ Telling Black girls to quiet down or describing them as rude when in fact they are not really showing either behavior	▶ You can't be trusted. You might be dangerous. ▶ Assertive Boys of Color are dangerous and likely to steal or do wrong; assertive white boys are confident. ▶ Girls of Color, or Black girls, are loud, defiant, and obnoxious.

THEMES	MICROAGGRESSION EXAMPLES	UNDERLYING MESSAGE
Denial of Individual Racism/Sexism/ Heterosexism A statement made when bias is denied	▶ Saying, "I can't be racist, some of my best friends are Black." ▶ Saying, "My sister has a disability, so I have no prejudice against people with disabilities." ▶ Saying, "I'm not homophobic, that was just a joke." ▶ Saying, "As a woman, I deal with sexism and know what the heterosexism you experience is like." ▶ Saying to a Student of Color "Are you sure you were being excluded because of racism?"	▶ Your oppression is no different than my oppression. ▶ Denies the personal experience of individuals who experience bias
Gender Stereotyping and Sexist Language Binary expectations of men and women	▶ Use of the pronoun "he" to refer to all people ▶ Asking students to do gender specific roles, like, "I need two strong boys to carry these boxes," or, "Could a few girls plan the refreshments for our party?" ▶ Ridiculing and excluding or allowing others to ridicule or exclude for not conforming to gender norms in terms of dress, interests, personality, and behaviors	▶ Male experience is universal. Female experience is invisible. ▶ There is a particular way to be male and a particular way to be female.

THEMES	MICROAGGRESSION EXAMPLES	UNDERLYING MESSAGE
Heterosexist Stereotyping and Language Terms that exclude or degrade LGBTQIA+ persons	▶ Heterosexual students using the word "gay" in place of "stupid" or "undesirable" ▶ Referring only to moms and dads when discussing adult caregivers ▶ Saying trans students are "strange" or "confused" about their gender identity	▶ LGBTQIA+ categories and partnerships are not recognized and/or demeaned. ▶ Men who do not fit male stereotypes are inferior.
Myth of Meritocracy Assumption that all groups have equal opportunity and that there is a level playing field; therefore, success or failure is due to individual effort and attributes; "blaming the victim"	▶ Saying, "Everyone has equal opportunities for achievement." ▶ Saying, "America is the land of opportunity." ▶ Saying, "You must not be trying hard enough."	▶ Your marginalized status or experiences with inequality don't matter.
Myth of Reverse Racism Statements which deny that white people have systemic privileges People of Color do not	▶ Saying, "Affirmative action is racist." ▶ Saying, "Reverse racism occurs a lot." ▶ Saying, "People of Color are racist, too!" ▶ Saying, "It's tough to be a white man these days."	▶ If People of Color get something, they must have gotten it because of affirmative action or because of reverse racism on the part of the bestowers. People of Color get away with racism and white people don't.

THEMES	MICROAGGRESSION EXAMPLES	UNDERLYING MESSAGE
Pathologizing Cultural Values/Communication Styles Assuming that certain groups are abnormal, deviant or pathological; assuming dominant cultural norms are correct and superior	▶ Saying to an African-American person, "You speak really well. You sound white." ▶ Asking, "Why do they have to be so loud/so quiet/dress like that?" ▶ Not putting a person with a disability in a front-line position ▶ Saying, "That food smells really funny."	▶ Assimilate to dominant culture. The dominant culture is better. ▶ There is no room for difference.
Second-Class Citizen Seeing certain groups as less worthy, less important, less deserving, inferior or invisible; people get excluded, ignored, or discriminated against	▶ Not wanting to sit by someone because of his/her color ▶ Setting low expectations for students from particular groups or neighborhoods, such as being surprised that Latinx or African American families can afford to live in a particular community and attend certain schools ▶ Tending to call on male students more frequently than female ones ▶ Assigning projects that ignore differences in socioeconomic class status and inadvertently penalize students with fewer financial resources	▶ You don't belong. ▶ You are a lesser being. ▶ What you have to say is not important.

Adapted from "Microaggressions" by Diane Goodman and "Tool: Recognizing Microaggressions and the Messages They Send" by Edith Ng. Original source: Sue, Derald Wing, *Microaggressions in Everyday Life: Race, Gender, and Sexual Orientation*, Wiley & Sons, 2010.

Get to Know Each Other

Creating positive relationships requires carving out time for relationship-building. Because teachers are under so much pressure to address academic content, it can feel like there is no time for learning, but, as Tyrone showed in Section 2, investing heavily in relationship-building activities pays off in academic achievement. Many students do not want to make themselves vulnerable by being truly known in school, so we need to take the first step.

Greet Each Student

Greeting students by name as they walk into the classroom every day seems obvious and yet many teachers still do not do it. Students need to know we see them as individuals and value the unique contribution they make to our classroom. If we do not greet each student, we risk letting a student feel overlooked, and that can start a negative pattern that can last the entire year. The first few minutes of class are crucial to setting the tone for the day. Ask quick questions like "How was your weekend?" or "How are you today?" and make positive noticing statements like "I love your shirt" or "I like your new haircut" or "You have got good energy today." Affirming our students reinforces their self-esteem and self-efficacy and ultimately how they feel about learning.

> *Many students do not want to make themselves vulnerable by being truly known in school, so we need to take the first step.*

A recent viral video shows one unique way of greeting students. Barry White Jr., a North Carolina teacher, cocreated joyful handshakes with his students (ABC News n.d.). In Kyra D. Gaunt's book *The Games Black Girls Play: Learning the Ropes from Double Dutch to Hip Hop*, Tashira Halyard (co-founder of the Black Girls Hand Games project in Washington, DC) explains that hand games can be an important way to build rapport because they "were a major factor in how we experienced the world as black girls." Gaunt says that for many Black girls, games are a way to "learn the rules of black social identity and musical practice" (2006). Such approaches can be powerful, and recess or before or after school can be a great time to invite, notice, and maybe even participate in this kind of activity.

Although it may not be realistic to do this with every student—a high school teacher can have as many as 150 students—
unique handshakes can be used to acknowledge students who need
a little more attention. And that is OK. Relationship-building is
idiosyncratic, based on the context. Choose options based on both
who your students are and who you are. You might try Tanya's
greeting—"Good morning, [Ms./Mr. Student's Last Name]"—to
establish a community of adults and mutual respect.

And, as powerful as culturally specific greetings can be, it
is also important to bear in mind that context and authenticity
matter. Cross-cultural exchanges are important but not to the point
of cultural appropriation. For example, a white teacher might use
African American Vernacular to connect with his Black students by
showing that he is familiar with youth culture. Instead of strength-
ening his bond with these students, he is ignoring their individual
identities by assuming all Black students will respond positively
to culturally specific colloquial phrases. A teacher should never
assume students' interests based on their appearance. Our job is
to learn about our students, not to assume, and to find ways to
connect with them based on their individual interests. Consider
this example instead: a white female teacher encourages her Black
female students' talents in stepping by inviting them to create an
afterschool club that will be featured in school performances. She
defines her role very clearly—she is not the expert or a partici-
pant, but the adult who supervises the after-school space and helps
navigate the bureaucracy of participation in school events. Addi-
tional examples of cultural respect versus cultural appropriation
can help guide us in making the right choice. Instead of guessing
what popular music students like and incorporating that into your
teaching for "relevance," consider asking students what music they
like and encourage them to teach you about the genres and artists
as well as to see if they can make connections to curriculum. If you
have students in your classroom who speak languages other than
English, consider asking them for assistance with words, phrases,
and sentences in those languages. This shows all students that
knowing languages other than English is an asset and that you
are not always the expert but sometimes a learner. Consciously
avoiding cultural appropriation shows students that we know and
respect them.

Community Cultural Wealth Inquiry

More often than we like, the empty vessel metaphor operates in our interactions with students: unconsciously, we behave as if students bring nothing of value into school and that they acquire their value by how much we fill them up with the conventional curriculum and expected behaviors of U.S. schooling. Yes, we might ask them about their interests, communities, and families, but do we see the information they share as reflecting valuable skills and understandings? Can we help them see that those skills and understandings are an asset, a kind of wealth, that overlaps and intertwines with their school learning in meaningful ways? Scholar Tara Yosso's Community Cultural Wealth Model (Yosso 2005) names six kinds of community cultural capital that students bring to school. Teachers can use these categories and the questions created by Angela Locks to identify opportunities for students to name and use their community cultural capital in school. (See Figure 3.4.)

> Yosso's approach fits within a culturally responsive model. For more details on the research behind this work, see Section 2, pages 20–22.

Student Interest Survey

An interest survey is a tool that can be shared between teacher and student. Giving this as students' first homework assignment is a great way to show students that you are eager to learn about them. Feel free to share some of your answers to the survey as a way of showing students that your classroom is a place where people's real selves are welcome. When given at the beginning of the year, the survey can help create a first impression of the student as created *by* the student. Who does the student want the teacher to know they are? Those choices of self-representation are important. As educator Sara Ahmed says, "We often ask kids to put themselves in someone else's shoes before we give them the opportunity to voice what it is like to be in their own shoes" (2018).

FIGURE 3.4 Community Cultural Capital Inquiries

Kinds of Community Cultural Capital	Teacher Inquiry	Classroom Opportunities
Aspirational Capital Defined by Yosso as the "hopes and dreams" that students have	▶ How are we supporting the maintenance and growth of students' aspirations? ▶ What assumptions do we have about our students' aspirations? ▶ Do teachers query students about their aspirations?	Ask students to write about their aspirations and then investigate one of those aspirations in an individual study or even a collaborative project if several students share an interest and want to explore it together. Model and encourage a range of aspirations outside those typically welcomed in academia too—including but not limited to character traits (generous, adventurous), creative ideas (singer, game developer) and lofty aspirations (end world hunger, give books to everyone).
Linguistic Capital The various language and communication skills students bring with them to school. Yosso further defines this form of capital by discussing the role of storytelling, particularly for Students of Color	▶ How are we supporting the language and communication strengths of our students? ▶ To what degree do courses utilize inclusive pedagogical practices?	Use writing workshop to explore oral storytelling. Make a conscious and transparent choice to use storytelling as a teaching method for important concepts beyond writing, such as illustrating a mathematical or scientific concept, and invite students to do the same. Consider bringing in a professional storyteller, having students name the techniques used, and then using them to perform their own oral storytelling.

Kinds of Community Cultural Capital	Teacher Inquiry	Classroom Opportunities
Familial Capital Students' extended familial and community networks	▶ How do we recognize and help students draw on wisdom, values, and stories from their home communities? ▶ How do we create environments that honor and invite families to participate?	Use home visits and student home surveys to gather information on families and their interest in skill sharing in school. For an example of how one first-grade teacher used familial capital for curriculum ideas, see "From Tanya's Classroom: Chiara" on page 58 of this section. Mention family strengths regularly in class discussions and lessons, underlining the strengths families provide students.
Social Capital Students' "peers and other social contacts" and emphasizes how students use these contacts to navigate the world	▶ How do we help students stay connected to their community and peers?	Consider project-based learning in collaboration with community organizations. Encourage students to create peer groups, both in and outside of school, to investigate and identify potential projects. Set up and regularly provide opportunities for students to teach to and learn from each other. Many schools have taken the EdCamp model (The EdCamp Foundation 2014) as an end-of-study celebration, asking students to volunteer to teach each other.

Kinds of Community Cultural Capital	Teacher Inquiry	Classroom Opportunities
Navigational Capital Students' skills and abilities to navigate institutions, with an emphasis on how they are empowered to maneuver within unsupportive or hostile environments	▶ How do we help students navigate our institutions? Interactions with teachers/faculty? Interactions with student-support staff? Their peers? ▶ How willing are we to acknowledge that our institutions, both their structures and cultures, have a history of being, and may still in many ways be, unsupportive and/or hostile to our students and their communities?	Invite school staff into classroom for celebrations and activities to give students opportunity to develop relationships with staff beyond problem-solving contexts. Explore present day inequities through classroom discussions and writing, as in the student journals from Chris Hass' class on page 60 of this section. Do regular "audits" with students of the systems they engage with regularly. Ask the students to set up the criteria and then study the systems for evidence of inequity, inclusion, or other features. Candidates for audit might include: topics/characters/ authors in classroom library, historical figures included (or excluded) in curriculum, representation in school art and photos, among others.

Kinds of Community Cultural Capital	Teacher Inquiry	Classroom Opportunities
Resistance Capital Founded in the experiences of Communities of Color securing equal rights and collective freedom; this historical legacy of resistance leaves Students of Color particularly well prepared to solve challenging social problems	▸ How do we support students who are committed to engaging in and serving their home communities (however they define these)? ▸ What opportunities do we provide students in and outside of the classroom to prepare them for participation in a diverse democracy?	Include articles from local newspapers on relevant issues in reading workshop. For high school, consider starting or ending each class with an "in the news" segment where students read and discuss an article reflecting these issues. Be sure to create dialogue around their agency and potential actions that can be supported in class as well as outside of school. Tell resistance stories from their families or community regularly. If you chose to do a curriculum, environment, or materials audit, guide and encourage students to create an action plan to combat any negative discoveries. Stand back from savior complex service projects (coat drives, can drives) and instead encourage students to study the system that caused the need and angle service projects toward resistance or system-dismantling projects as service.

Adapted from "Summary of Yosso's Cultural Wealth Model" by Angela Locks. Reprinted with permission from Angela Locks.

There are a wide variety of student interest surveys available. Figure 3.5 is one that we created and used in classrooms, but we encourage you to adapt it to reflect what you want to know about your students.

FIGURE 3.5 Student Interest Survey

- Who is your all-time favorite teacher? What kind of activities did that teacher do that kept you actively engaged?
- What do you expect (want) to learn this year from your teacher/teachers?
- What do you like or enjoy about your community or neighborhood?
- If you could fix or change one thing in your neighborhood or community what would it be?
- If you could fix or correct one global problem, what would it be?
- What are you usually doing when you are the happiest person ever?
- What is something that really makes you upset or sad?
- WhatcanIdoasyourteachertoassurethatyouwillbesuccessfulthisyear?
- What do you like most about school?
- What do you dislike most about school?
- What are some things that your "least favorite" teacher ever did in order to earn that title?
- If you could be the principal for a day, what changes would you make within the school?
- If you could be the teacher for a day, what changes would you make within the classroom?
- Do you enjoy completing your assignments alone or with a group?
- Tell me about your relationships at home (siblings, cousins, neighbors). Where do you fit? What are you like when you are at home?
- Tell me about your dreams and aspirations.
- What are two or three things you are really good at doing?
- What are three words that you would use to describe yourself?
- What is something about you that you wish others knew about you?

Of course, a student interest survey only works if we hold onto what students share in meaningful ways. After collecting and reading student surveys, we could use the survey to:

- identify some shared topics of interest in the class and invite students to brainstorm some ways the class might explore those interests throughout the year

- identify opportunities throughout the year to explore individual interests

- ask students to consider what they wrote and use it to brainstorm a set of classroom goals

- use the survey to launch individual student conferences that discuss what the student wants to happen as a learner that year and wants from you as a teacher.

Using surveys can help the teacher address specific concerns immediately, as Tanya explains in her classroom reflection.

From Tanya's Classroom

Chiara

I have become privy to a lot of pertinent information about students through surveys. One year, Chiara described herself with the following words: *stupid, ugly, dumb.* My heart broke for her when I learned this was not a particularly bad day but her daily sense of self. Chiara shared that her mom had recently lost her job and was struggling. I was able to connect her with support services for her family and a school counselor. My ongoing work was to help build Chiara's confidence and to make sure things were going better for her family. All this was kept private, but thanks to the survey my support of Chiara began on the very first day of school.

Dialogue/Classroom Journals

Dialogue journals are notebooks that teachers and students use to write letters back and forth to each other. The journals keep communication open throughout the year and help deepen the teacher–student relationship over time. (See Figure 3.6.) For many students it is much easier to write their thoughts on paper rather than say what they are feeling out loud. (See Figures 3.7a–c.) Although for the most part teachers should let these journals be open-ended and not use prompts as a significant part of writing instruction, there are limited occasions when a thoughtfully selected prompt can be useful for the purpose of relationship-building. The "three wishes" prompt in the student example included here allows students to identify their aspirational capital (Yosso 2005).

FIGURE 3.6 *Guidelines for Dialogue Journals*

- Suggest possible topics but invite students to write about what feels most pressing or interesting to them.
- Set aside 5–10 minutes each day at the beginning or end of the school day or class period for students to write.
- Let students know that you may not be able to read every entry and to tag with a sticky the entries that are most important to read that week.
- Make sure you write a response to at least one journal entry each week. This can be half a journal page.
- Grade students on their journals for completion, not length, content, grammar, or substance. Writing to reflect is worthy academic and personal work and deserves to be recognized. Always focus on the positives and never focus on the negatives and/or mechanics of the journal. No one wants to see their personal letters marked up with a red pen, but you can take mental note of lessons you might teach based on needs noticed in journal entries.
- Consider writing the first entry yourself in response to students' interest surveys.

FIGURES 3.7a, 3.7b, 3.7c *Student Journals*

My family enjoys having Thanksgiving because we always give Thanks to each other. On Thanksgiving all of my family goes to my grandmas house and my papa cooks a big meal like turkey, Mac n Cheese, Chicken Dressing, and etc. Also on Thanksgiving me and my cousins go outside and run around and play with each other. At the end of the day, we spend the night with our Aunties.

Xiy'lah, I love how your family gives Thanks to/for each other during Thanksgiving. I would love to add this tradition to my family's traditions because it is always nice to be appreciated by your loved ones.

How do you all make this happen? Do you sit in a circle and take turns or do you do it at the table before, after, or during your meal?

If I was to meet a magical fairy who would give me three wishes, my first wish is that the whole word didn't have violance. I choose this because in our world there is many people violance and that causes them to kill which is bad. My second wish that people have love for others. I choose this because many people don't have Love for others then they get sad or furious and they can hurt other people and that can be bad. Then my last wish would be that people can get money to get whatever they want whatever they need. I choose this because many people don't have money to buy what they need and since they are poor they can't get a job to earn money.

Raleigh
My Grandma was in the goverment She was around the taliban in Afganisan. The People in the Goverment Had a Partner and had to look out for each other When the bombs whould be let down. The People in the goverment whould have to go in fox holes to hide from bombs and the talidan

Classroom journals can be a way to get to support students' curiosity about specific content, too. Elementary school teacher Chris Hass, at the Center for Inquiry in Columbia, South Carolina, invites his students to record questions in content journals (math, science, social studies, language arts, and social justice) that students can choose to inquire about in morning meeting, as independent inquiry, or collectively as a class. (See Figures 3.8a–b.)

FIGURES 3.8a, 3.8b *Classroom Journals*

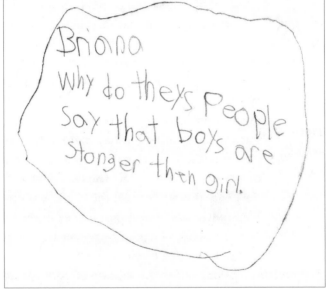

Writing to reflect is an essential academic behavior and life skill but the journals can become meaningless to students if you do not engage with them in some way. For dialogue journals, write a response to each student at least every two weeks. Dialogue journals can also create opportunities for larger, important conversations. When a student writes about something that could become a whole-class activity, ask the student if you can use their journal entry in class. You do not have to read the entry if the student does not want you to, but you could say something like, "Brianna really got me thinking when she wrote in her journal about . . ." Shared classroom journals become most effective when students know that every day is an opportunity to explore what they wonder. This is easier to do in an elementary school morning meeting but can also happen in the first 5–10 minutes of a middle or high school class.

Share Personal Details with Students

Teachers need to share themselves with students but have their emotional needs met elsewhere. A teacher's willingness to be known by their students is as important as knowing their students, but what do you share and what do you keep private? That is personal of course and context specific, but it is worth saying that teachers should not expect their emotional needs to be met by a student. This expectation is what makes self-care so important to teachers' health and professional endurance. We are often in the double bind of using up so much emotional, physical, and social energy on our students during our day that we often do not have interest, time, or energy to socialize outside of work. That is not OK. The only way we will have the strength to meet the emotional needs of our students is to meet our own emotional needs *outside of school.* Every teacher must prioritize consistent self-care. Because the profession of teaching is inherently centered on selfless giving, we must be unapologetic in taking care of ourselves physically, mentally, emotionally, and spiritually.

> *Because the profession of teaching is inherently centered on selfless giving, we must be unapologetic in taking care of ourselves physically, mentally, emotionally, and spiritually.*

Our relationship with a student is defined by the student's needs, not ours. Our students need to know and understand that we are human and may have endured life challenges like theirs. But we have seen some teachers work so hard to establish positive relationships with their students that they end up sharing details about their lives that one would normally only tell an adult friend. We must maintain professional boundaries. This can be especially important for teenagers who are reaching adulthood and can be unclear about where the boundaries are between a seventeen-year-old student and a twenty-five-year-old teacher. It is our job to show that we care and are reliable without misleading students to think that our relationship is identical to what they have with their peers or family members.

Keep your personal social media accounts private. We are not friends with students or their families on social media. We state this as a policy on the first day of school so that no one personalizes the decision. Of course, you might choose to create a social media presence solely for your professional identity as teacher or for your class, but keep your personal and professional social media separate. (See Figure 3.11 for ideas on making yourself accessible online to families and students.)

> *We must maintain professional boundaries.*

Although we strongly believe that many decisions depend on context, the following are some useful guidelines for sharing personal details with students.

Share Personal Details with Purpose

■ **Details that show you are passionate about a variety of things.** Do you like old movies, hip-hop, comic books, sports, cooking, parkour, attending religious services, video games, lectures, volunteering? Let students know. Students might not think your hobbies are interesting. That is not the point. The point is to give them examples of what being interested in the world can look like. This also helps students see you as a whole person, not just as a teacher. Do not just tell students about your interests; incorporate them into your teaching when the connection feels right. Use a comic book excerpt to talk about character or representation. Use a favorite song to talk about text structure. Start a class by sharing an idea you recently learned that you cannot stop thinking about. It is your passion and engagement with the world that you want them to see. They will find their own interests (especially if you can create time for them to explore these within the curriculum), but the more diverse examples they are exposed to, the greater the chance that they will pursue their own.

■ **Stories that show you dealing with embarrassment and failure.** Students often believe they are alone in their imperfections, self-doubt, and moments of embarrassment, and this can cause them to isolate themselves and become frozen in their difficulty. One of the most important things we as trusted adults can teach them is that struggle and failure are normal and shared by everyone. For example, when we were teenagers, we sometimes stood up for other kids being bullied and sometimes did not. We both felt a lot of self-loathing for not consistently being an ally to other kids and were not able to reconcile that until we were older. So, we talk about this with students to acknowledge the difficulty firsthand. This has prompted deep discussions about peer pressure, personal safety, and collaborative identification of strategies that might have served us (and would serve them) better. Or it could be helpful to talk to students about when you or your family experienced a difficult time, such as a move to a new neighborhood, financial hardship, parents separating, or the loss of a loved one. We want to help students learn not to be defeated by the inevitable difficulties they will encounter. The earlier that students understand that they will always be in a constant state of becoming, the less time they will waste wondering why they are not perfect yet.

■ **Stories that model constructive and faulty decision-making.** It can be useful for students to see how we teach ourselves to be metacognitive about decision-making. From something little, like trying to eat better or to be more considerate of a challenging person, to larger questions, like struggling with paying for college and deciding what to do next. Humor often works. Often students feel that they would be much more competent than our ridiculous examples, which in and of itself is good.

■ **Stories that explain systemic injustice.** Our society struggles with the myth of meritocracy and that we can and should pull ourselves up by our own bootstraps. We believe that is a toxic lie meant to keep power and privilege in the hands of some and not others. No one succeeds on their own; some are born with privilege and some are unjustly marked by society as undeserving. And to be clear, those who are born into or with privilege also can work hard and have struggles. Some reject the idea of privilege because they believe that they have put lots of time into reaching goals. This can be quite true. However, the reality is that those in positions of privilege have more advantages and opportunities compared with those who are not in privileged positions and who may be working just as hard—or in some cases even harder. Young people see and experience prejudice and discrimination at very early ages, so avoiding discussions around racism, homophobia, xenophobia, misogyny, and discrimination can undermine our relationships with students. As education scholar Paul Gorski explains,

> For the research that argues for this necessary work, see Section 2, page 28.

> *No one succeeds on their own; some are born with privilege and some are unjustly marked by society as undeserving.*

> "treating individual traumas without naming systemic injustice means schools don't just risk leaving some traumas unrecognized; it means they risk retraumatizing students." True trauma-informed work, he says, must recognize and address the *school's* role in creating or re-creating trauma. In fact, that should be the starting point. Students who are experiencing trauma can be retraumatized in school through poorly chosen readings, activities and assignments. Gorski offers an example: "I often hear from students who are learning about racism in the past tense," he says. "For instance, they are reading *To Kill a Mockingbird* and learning about what it was like for people of color 'back then.' At the same time, they are experiencing racism in school and in their communities in the present tense. It's disorienting and damaging when students aren't given the opportunity to explore these injustices in their present communities." (Gaffney 2019)

We have a professional and ethical duty not only to acknowledge systemic oppression but also to work to eliminate it as an obstacle to students' success and well-being. Students need to understand the limiting judgments of bigotry so they can avoid placing it on others, can minimize personalizing the impact on themselves, and can find strength in alternative narratives. To that end, those stories should not only be based on our personal experience alone but call out patterns of identity (the powerful and oppressed), the complexity of identity (that people are rarely one fixed trait), and how people construct identity in a variety of circumstances. We can look to the experiences of characters; authors, mathematicians, and scientists; historical figures; as well as events in the news to find examples beyond ourselves, ones that represent the identities of our students and of people in the world in diverse, substantive ways. The stories we share of noticing this narrative of oppression and finding more true and meaningful ones map a safer path for our students. To explore more, visit the websites in the resource box.

> *We have a professional and ethical duty not only to acknowledge systemic oppression but also to work to eliminate it as an obstacle to students' success and well-being.*

Resources for Talking About Systems of Oppression with Students

Teaching Tolerance **https://www.tolerance.org/**

Rethinking Schools **https://www.rethinkingschools.org/**

Education for Liberation Network **https://edliberation.org**

Raising Race Conscious Students **http://www.raceconscious.org/**

Center for Racial Justice in Education
http://centerracialjustice.org/resources/resources-for-talking-about-race-racism-and-racialized-violence-with-kids/

■ **Stories that emphasize connection and responsibility to others.**
The more students understand that they can expect help from
us and their classmates, the more willing they are to receive
it. Every day students are inundated with stories of takers—
people who follow the American story of individualism to the
point where they no longer recognize anyone else as human be-
sides themselves or their small group. Students need antidotes
to that endless drip of poison. By sharing stories of when we
were helped by and helped others, we define an expectation for
our classroom community and invite students toward positive
connections that can help them navigate difficulty and injustice.

Sometimes the decision about what to share is not always
clear-cut. For example, historically, LGBTQIA+ teachers were
expected to keep their sexual identity private. We now understand
how important LGBTQIA+ awareness is for students, particularly
students coming to terms with their own gender identity and sexual
orientation. Thankfully, some LGBTQIA+ teachers decided to start
sharing their stories, their struggles, and their pride in being their
authentic selves. It is up to the individual teacher to share what
feels appropriate. Whether you mention your partner or do not is a
personal decision. Mention your kids or do not. Know that certain
boundaries, such as more adult details about relationships, should
stay private, regardless of sexual orientation. To explore more, visit
the websites in the resource box.

Resources for Talking About Gender and Sexual Identity with Students

HRC Foundation's Welcoming Schools
http://www.welcomingschools.org/

Teaching Tolerance's Gender & Sexual Identity
https://www.tolerance.org/topics/gender-sexual-identity

Gender Spectrum's Resources page
https://www.genderspectrum.org/resources/

Teachers who shy away from revealing aspects of their identity should not be condemned. Everyone is on their own journey and forcing someone to be vulnerable is disrespectful. If one

Everyone is on their own journey and forcing someone to be vulnerable is disrespectful.

chooses to share, it is important to understand that colleagues, administrators, students, and parents may respond in unfavorable or hurtful ways. The individual needs to make an informed decision and protect themselves. As Black educators, we know how important our presence is in schools. We carry the burden and responsibility of not only being an adult role model but also of being representative of our racial group. For us, sharing is not a choice; our racial identities are in plain sight. We choose to focus on details from our lives that celebrate Black people, history, and culture as well as intentionally sharing details about ourselves that challenge stereotyping. We understand that some Teachers of Color are uncomfortable or unwilling to take on this work. The burden around racial literacy should not belong to Teachers of Color alone. White teachers, too, must create spaces for racial dialogue and develop their own racial literacy, and they need to choose a position of inquiry rather than always looking for Teachers of Color to respond to the needs of Students of Color. Letting students know what you do not know and want to learn can be a big step in building relational trust. Uncertain? It is always useful to talk through what feels right with a trusted colleague. If you do not have one yet, find one. You need to draw on strength from others to be able to give to others.

Regular Communication with Families and Caregivers

Connecting to families and caregivers is an essential but easily overlooked responsibility of teachers. Our teaching days are so full that the connection often feels like a "nice to do" item on our long list of "necessary now" items. Because of that, we are often in a reactive stance, only reaching out to parents and caregivers when something is wrong. When we establish patterns like this,

But That   69

it is unsurprising families and caregivers are reluctant to respond. And, when they do not respond to conference invitations or show up to Open House night, we can nurture bias. Those biases can then affect our relationship with students. When a caregiver does not respond to our phone calls or emails, we have to keep that separate from our relationship with the student. It gives us some information, yes, but it does not necessarily tell us who the student is. As we learn about students' families, we cannot equate difference with deficit.

For the research that shows how necessary positive home communication and family relationship-building is, see Section 2, pages 17–18.

As Tyrone noted in Section 2, the worst thing we can do for a student is feel pity for them. Pity is not empathy; it is a deficit perspective on students' identity. It is important to understand that although we might see disengaged families, we cannot assume we understand why. Our job is not to judge but to listen, learn, and, if possible, to help. Parents or caregivers may want to attend events but school hours conflict with most people's work hours, and evening activities can, too. It is important also not to assume that a student is being raised by their parents. Some students are in foster care and any assumptions we make about their lives at home—whether we talk about parents, not knowing a student is separated from theirs, or whether we adopt a "poor student" approach because of their foster status—can be

Our job is not to judge but to listen, learn, and, if possible, to help.

damaging. It is essential that we learn who our students' families are prior to communicating with families and communicate in such a way that no students feel excluded or marked by difference. Early in the year, teachers should discuss the variety of ways a "family" can exist so that every student sees themselves in that shared class definition.

Equally important is to make sure that the line of communication between families and school goes in two directions—that teachers and students learn from families as much, if not more, than families learn from us. As Luis Moll's Funds of Knowledge (1992) model illustrates, families have worthy knowledge and expertise. There are a variety of ways you can gather this information from families and students and use it, but here is one example of a first-grade teacher from Washington state, who gathered funds of knowledge from a home visit to Ruby's family and how that might inform her classroom work. Ruby is an emerging multilingual student from El Salvador. (See Figure 3.9.)

Usually teachers do "getting to know you and your family" activities at the beginning of the year, but consider how your communication can be ongoing as in the following examples.

FIGURE 3.9 *Funds of Knowledge: Information Gathering and Classroom Applications*

FUNDS OF KNOWLEDGE	HOME/COMMUNITY PRACTICES	CLASSROOM APPLICATIONS
Economics	When Ruby's parents lived in El Salvador, the currency was different. They had saved their old money in a small box.	We could use this in math. Money in math is very common, but using different currencies would bring in the family's funds of knowledge, especially if we have other cultures in our classroom that we may not know about.
Geography	There were a lot of maps around their home. I saw a large world map of South and North America. I also saw small maps of El Salvador on key chains. Ruby's mother also brought out a towel that resembled the Salvadorian flag.	This could be used in social studies. We could look at cities in Washington and take it a step farther and move from each continent and have table groups look more closely at cities in specific continents or regions.
Politics	Ruby's family had Direct TV so they got to watch news that came right out of El Salvador. Her mother and father even recorded the news so they would not miss it when it came on.	We could use this in social studies. Young students most likely will not be very interested in the news, but they could have an assignment that has them work with their parents to choose a topic or find a story in the news that is relevant to today's dates.

FUNDS OF KNOWLEDGE	HOME/COMMUNITY PRACTICES	CLASSROOM APPLICATIONS
Agriculture	In the back yard, Ruby showed me where her father would be planting tomatoes this summer.	We could use this idea to create a classroom garden or talk about plant growth in science.
Technology	Ruby's home was full of technology. They had a TV in almost every room and they had lots of computers throughout the home as well.	We could use technology during math with online math games. We could also have the students begin typing their own stories on the computers. I do think we should start off with a typing lesson beforehand. Or we could even find sorting games to introduce the different kinds of technology.
Religion	Ruby's family is Catholic. Throughout the home there were a lot of paintings and portraits of Jesus Christ. They also had gold jewelry with angels and other figures on them. In Ruby's room, she showed me a Rosario from the Bible she and her mother had written down together.	For social studies, we could compare Christianity with other prominent religions around the world and research different religions and places of worship in our city. For math, we could compare numbers of practicing members of the different religions around the world.
Language	The home is Spanish dominant, but her mother does speak a bit of English and her brothers and sisters speak English fluently. One photo of her mother and sister has a heading which says, "Mi Familia." Most of the home posters/writing/pictures are in Spanish. She did explain to me that the accent or dialect in El Salvador is different than your usual Mexican accent.	For language arts, we could compare different dialects of Spanish and read texts from different regions of Latin America to see how those dialects are represented. I could invite Ruby's mom to talk about El Salvador and her experiences speaking Spanish in the U.S.

FUNDS OF KNOWLEDGE	HOME/COMMUNITY PRACTICES	CLASSROOM APPLICATIONS
Cooking	Ruby's mother was cooking while I visited. She was in the process of making platanos con frijoles y cremo. I had never tried this before, so I knew it was one of their family's favorite recipes.	I could work on procedural vocabulary by having students work with their parents to write their favorite recipes. This would also apply to math by pointing out quantity words in addition to measurements.

Adapted from Funds of Knowledge Inventory Matrix by Office of Superintendent of Public Instruction/ Creative Commons Attribution License. Original materials may be freely accessed on the OSPI website.

Messages Home

Messages to families are a great tool for relationship-building. In addition to ongoing communication with all families, consider personalized communication to each family at least three times throughout the year: an introduction before school starts, a mid-year message celebrating what you have seen in the class and student so far, and an end-of-year message recognizing the growth of the student and what you have learned from them. If you are writing a letter, the mid- and end-of-year letters could be sent via email, although it can be nice for families to have a hard copy. Yes, this is easier to do when you teach K–5 and have no more than thirty students, but grades 6–12 teachers can do it, too, even with over 120 students. Try using Figure 3.10's letter guidelines.

FIGURE 3.10 *Family/Caregiver Introduction Letter Guidelines*

1. Address the envelope to the student, the letter to the student and family ("Dear Marcus and Family").

2. Introduce yourself. Keep it short but try to provide interesting details that really describe you as a teacher and human being.

3. Introduce the year. Give them a sneak peek at some exciting learning experiences they will have that year.

4. Show that you are eager to get to know the student and their family. Write a series of questions you have about that student that feel easy and invitational:

- What three words best describe you?
- What are three things that you do very well?
- Can you speak more than one language?
- What is your vision of a perfect day?
- What do you enjoy most about your family? (Consider inviting family members to teach something to the class during the school year.)

5. Send the letter in the middle of students' summer vacation and encourage them to write back and/or share examples of things they like to make. You might choose to include a self-addressed, stamped envelope to increase the likelihood they will. If you would rather not include your personal address, use the school's, just be sure to check your mail regularly after you have sent the letters.

Even if students do not respond, you have communicated that you are interested in them. If three letters seem too much right now, just try the summer letter and consider trying a midyear/end-of-year letter the following year. Figure 3.11 offers teaching tools to help you maintain ongoing family communication.

FIGURE 3.11 *Varieties of Ongoing Family Communication*

We usually send out two messages a week. Know that communication does not have to be via print. Consider a weekly YouTube video/podcast from you or text message updates (short and easy to consume).

Email/text families about important assignment due dates.

Although elementary teachers often do this, it is useful to do this for grades 6–12 families, too. Some schools use texting apps, which can be even more useful because most families look at their phones more often than email, and many of these apps (like Remind, Seesaw, and What's App) can translate English into different languages.

Each week throughout the year, send a positive message home about one student.

Keep a notebook or Word document open so that you can write something down throughout the school year as you notice it. You could call home, text, email. You can always do this more often as you notice great things, but start with an easy goal.

Email/text families about free/inexpensive local activities, student internships, or media programming that would be enriching for kids.

Local libraries often have great events that families do not know about. Often there are festivals, cultural celebrations, or community and historical events that take place. Some museums are free on a weekend day before noon. Let them know about great articles, books, documentaries, and websites. Encourage caregivers to consume media alongside students. Democratize enrichment.

Email/text families about socioemotional learning tips and resources, particularly ones that help families understand phases of student development.

It is important for caregivers and students to understand what normal struggle is as well as understand that there are tools and strategies to help them. Recommending interactive tutorial websites (Codecademy, Khan Academy, and Katacoda) and free parenting websites (PBS Kids and NBC Learn's Parent Toolkit) can be invaluable resources for parents and caregivers who are looking to support their learners, no matter the age.

Email/text families to acknowledge individual/community accomplishments.

Recently five of my students competed for a state championship football title in the recreation league of our city. For the first time in approximately thirty-five years, a team from our city would be playing in this championship game, so I sent out a Remind message to students and their families. It was not a celebration of just those five students but our community. Sending out these messages lets the students know that I care about them and what is going on in their lives outside of school.

Start a class website or blog.

Begin the year with a class website or blog (Google Classroom, Weebly, WordPress, etc.) where you can regularly post quick notes, flipped lessons, suggested resources, upcoming deadlines and events, and assignments. Depending on the platform you use, this site can also be used for students to work on group projects, share writing, and create their own tutorials for class content. Over time students can take over the upkeep and maintenance of the site, including writing blog entries and updating events.

Create a class social media presence.

If your students are old enough and active on social media, you might consider creating a class social media account that students and families can follow and participate in. Whether Twitter, Instagram, or something else, many students and their families are likely to follow these accounts and interact with them. Although it is important to take care to not include pictures of students' faces without their families' permission, there are many ways to document class events and current areas of study and offer resources for further learning.

Rethink Open House

The following Open House ideas in Figure 3.12 are tools to help you ensure contact with more families. The stronger the connection with families, the more successful the student in school. You may not get 100 percent attendance, but we guarantee these strategies will increase family participation.

FIGURE 3.12 *Open House Ideas*

Make translators available. What are the home languages spoken by your students? Find students, school, or family/community volunteers who can be present to assist nonnative English speakers if needed.

Provide free childcare. Childcare can be an issue for attendance. Consider creating a space where older students/volunteers provide free childcare. Put on a film or play games. Make the association with school fun for the younger students, too!

Make the open house a celebration of students, not just an information dump. Considering having students perform music/poetry and creating a gallery of student art and projects. Attendance will increase if you make it an occasion that celebrates students. To push this idea even further, consider how Open House might evolve into a celebration of the community of the school. How might families share their funds of knowledge with the community so that the gathering is truly transactional?

Provide useful family resources. In planning the Open House, include activities and resources useful to the whole family, like job fairs, heating, health, and food assistance. Identify the needs and interests of your particular community and see if you can support them. Often families do not know about the free activities available to their students through the school and their community. Consider gathering those together in one handout with activity representatives available to meet and talk with families. The more positive adult and peer connections a student has, the greater the chances for their life success.

Consider technology to connect. A more convenient way for schools to connect to parents and caregivers is through podcasts and live streaming online videos that allow adults and students to connect to the information from the comfort of their homes or jobs. Videotaping messages or information from teachers or administrators that require a simple click can reduce the heavy lift that some parents and caregivers may have when it comes to transportation to the school, student care, or simple fatigue from a full day of work. The more that schools can make information accessible and easier to connect, the better. Many schools have the technological infrastructure that easily transforms the way schools and families connect.

Provide a meal. Few things are more powerful for bringing people in and building community than breaking bread together. By offering a meal, perhaps furnished by local restaurants in exchange for a thank-you, we signal to families that we want to spend time with them and we understand that evening meals can be a scramble and a stress. Meals provide care as well as remove an obstacle to coming. If your school is located in an area where there are few if any restaurants, setting up tables and offering a potluck can also be a great way to make food a centerpiece.

Develop Every Student's Potential

Many students pass through school feeling like their potential as a unique human being is unseen. And they are not wrong. As Tyrone showed in Section 2, students from low-income backgrounds or Students of Color frequently receive the "poor student" approach from teachers. The "poor student" is steeped in a deficit-based belief that students do not have the intellectual capacity or emotional resources to handle challenging school work. Such approaches create irreparable damage to students' abilities to learn and undermine authentic relationships.

Teachers must have high expectations for every student. When a teacher allows a student to do less than what the student is capable of, the student will likely continue to do work that does not reflect their potential. That is not the student's fault; it is ours. We communicated that we expected less of them. To hold students accountable to their potential, teachers must really know their students. In some classrooms, students with disabilities are held to impossibly high standards and sometimes referred to as "lazy." So, the first step to student accountability is teacher inquiry. Why might this work not be as strong as it can be? We have to do the work of recognizing what the student can and cannot do *yet*. We need to recognize what a student needs to be able to do in order to reach that standard of high achievement today, tomorrow, and across the year so that we can see significant growth from our time spent together.

Use Figure 3.13 to help you self-evaluate and identify ways that you can shift from the "poor student" approach to an asset perspective on students' potential.

FIGURE 3.13 Shifting from a Deficit to Asset Perspective on Students' Potential

"POOR STUDENT" APPROACH	"CAPABLE STUDENT" APPROACH
Feels sorry for students because of challenging life circumstances	Empathizes with student, but still encourages student to believe that life circumstances do not define you; offers academic and emotional support

"POOR STUDENT" APPROACH	"CAPABLE STUDENT" APPROACH
Lowers expectations because the student cannot "handle" hard work	Recognizes students' needs but refuses to lower expectations; works with student on plan to meet academic goals
Provides students with "busywork" to help them experience success	Encourages and recognizes student progress and effort on challenging tasks
Allows disruptive behavior to be commonplace because the students cannot "control" themselves	Does not allow disruptive behavior to be an excuse; communicates clear expectations and is fair and firm with all students
Allows sloppy or inadequate work to be acceptable, and praises student for doing subpar work with minimal effort	Stresses to students that their personal best is always expected; no shortcuts are allowed; effort and care matter

In the following classroom reflection, Jaleel shares an example of inviting a student into greater participation through her strengths.

From Jaleel's Classroom

Kionna

Remember Kionna from Section 1? Because my early attempts to connect to Kionna were unsuccessful (the "invisible" student described in Section 1), I decided to take the one thing I did know—that she was a gifted artist—and turn it into a connection. As long as Kionna finished her work in class, she was free to doodle in her dialogue journal. The first few days, she did not seem interested but eventually she took me up on my offer. Giving her the space to do what she loved in class drew her more strongly into our community. I talked to her about the insight in her drawings and said that I would love to have that thinking present in our class discussions. Maybe she might be willing to try one comment in each class period? Although Kionna remained silent most of the class period, her participation did increase, and I did not want to push her beyond

To review Jaleel and Kionna's struggling relationship, see Section 1, page 8.

what felt comfortable for her. It is important to respect students' different ways of interacting; Kionna was an introvert. On my birthday, I found a poem addressed to me that expressed her appreciation for making her feel comfortable in class. Over time, Kionna started writing more in her journal and, as she wrote more, her academic skills began to improve. Although Kionna had been a high-performing student, I came to understand that her disengagement allowed us both not to see that she could do more.

Kionna's revealing of self and participation was slow—the pace was Kionna's, and not mine. In hindsight that is probably the most respectful thing I could offer. Not all students open up in the same way. Kionna taught me the importance of giving students time and a variety of ways to be known.

In our relationships with students, we sometimes forget that we are addressing not just the relationship between one teacher and one student but every relationship that student has had with teachers and in school. As teachers, we often inherit broken faith. When a student has passed through grade after grade without being taught the skills they need, they lose faith in school. It is our job to provide the evidence—the teaching and support—that will repair that broken faith. (See Figure 3.14 for strategies.)

Now let's see how Tanya learned to help repair one student's broken faith in her next classroom reflection.

FIGURE 3.14 Strategies for Repairing Broken Academic Faith

STRATEGY	POSSIBLE TEACHER LANGUAGE
Name the student's academic skills, both what the student can already do within the conventional curriculum and their existing transferrable life skills that can be applied to school.	"Marta, you are the kid in the class who knows what is going on with everyone. You know everyone's business and people want your advice. I am wondering if you could try to bring that to our peer conferring time in writing by . . . ?"

STRATEGY	POSSIBLE TEACHER LANGUAGE
Convey to students your belief in their ability to learn, even with difficult content.	"Yes, this is hard. You can do hard things."
Develop daily learning and/or behavior goals based on where the student is today and where they can be by the end of the day/class period. We need to re-earn students' trust by letting them see evidence of immediate and measurable success.	"Today I would like you to read up to the page you and your book club decided on and then jot a few thoughts down. How does that sound?"
Recognize the "just-right" amount of struggle for that student. Give them the opportunity to explore their limits but do not let them sit frustrated for an extended period. Figure out the bridge that will move them a little bit further that day.	"I know Mondays are hard for you. But today is an important Monday. Do you think you can stay with me for the first twenty minutes of class? Then, if that works out, you can take a break? Then come back and stay on task until the end?"
Give them tasks that are consistently challenging but within reach and let them know how you think it might go. The simple act of naming a challenging task and supporting them through it is a success that students can own, be it their first word problem, their first time writing beyond a paragraph or a page, their first time reading a chapter book or a book that is over 200 pages long.	"This is a really interesting equation. It is going to take a bit of time to do. But I know that you can and have done everything that it calls for. Do not be intimidated by the length. You have got this. Let me know when you think you are ready to share what you figured out."
Celebrate their success. Three, five, and ten months can often be good academic year benchmarks to identify what a student can now do that they could not before. They need to see that their time spent in school is always moving them forward.	"Look at you! We talked about you aiming to read a book a week. Look at this—we are only three months into school and you are already over that goal by one book! How does that feel?"

From Tanya's Classroom

David

Remember David from Section 1? After much reflection and conversation with some colleagues, I realized that I had neglected to connect David's behavior to his academic identity. I decided to experiment by really focusing on reframing his struggle with reading and giving him targeted work and feedback that helped him see how he was becoming a smarter, better reader each day. Although normally I make sure I do

To review Tanya and David's struggling relationship, see Section 1, pages 6–7.

reading conferences with different students each day, for the first several weeks, I made sure I had at least a three-minute reading conference with David almost every day using the strategies for repairing broken academic faith and moving from deficit to asset perspectives. I came to think that David had initiated his disruptive behaviors in school because of his academic struggle and that teachers had consistently responded to the behaviors and not his learning needs.

This did not make everything better. David's disruptive behavior was an ingrained response to struggle in academics and relationships. However, his disruptive behaviors became less frequent and I became less reactive to them. Both of us had found some degree of relationship success through our conversations around reading. I was extra conscious of giving him choice in what he wanted to read, in how he thought he might work on his reading that day, and in asking him to self-assess his own growth before I offered him my thoughts. When David came up with a great plan for reading that day, I celebrated his insights by offering it to the class as a possibility during independent work. Through his past experiences at school, David had managed to erase his academic identity through behavior, and I was trying to invite it back in with gentle care and attention.

At the end of the year, we did not have a perfect relationship: we still got frustrated with each other more than either of us would have liked. But we both knew that we could show up for the relationship in positive ways, and David was reading almost on grade level.

Create Opportunities for Peer Collaboration

As Tyrone explained in Section 2, teachers need to take responsibility for students' positive peer relationships. Peer connection is an essential human need and yet too many teachers do not create meaningful opportunities for it to happen in school. When we do not make time and space for our relationship with students, we communicate that no relationships matter in this

For the research on peer relationships, see Section 2, pages 18–20.

space. So many of the disruptive behaviors we see in classrooms, particularly among boys, comes from them being denied enough time to connect with their peers. When we say that relationships matter in this classroom and plan for peer connection, we meet a basic human need and avoid some of the disruptive feedback students show when they do not get what they need. A high school principal in a low-socioeconomic-status school with a 90 percent reported trauma rate recently shared that the more opportunities students had for peer collaboration, the lower the incidence of trauma-related behaviors in his school. The more peer collaboration belongs to the students, the more effective it will be.

Project-Based Learning

The student survey and journals we shared earlier all provide easy launching points for peer collaboration through project-based learning. In high-quality project-based learning:

■ Students learn deeply, think critically, and strive for excellence.

■ Students work on projects that are meaningful and relevant to their culture, their lives, and their future.

■ Students' work is publicly displayed, discussed, and critiqued.

■ Students collaborate with other students in person or online and/or receive guidance from adult mentors and experts.

■ Students use a project management process that enables them to proceed effectively from project initiation to completion.

■ Students reflect on their work and their learning throughout the project (High Quality Project Based Learning n.d.).

A variety of free project-based learning resources for planning and implementing your own units based on the interests of students in your class can be found at https://hqpbl.org/resources/.

Depending on the grade or subject you teach, these projects could be connected to your curriculum (local response to climate change, Little Free Library) or something more open-ended (documentary making, school beautification). The idea is that students would be working together for a real purpose. Whether this purpose is framed by you or brainstormed by your students is less important than giving students an opportunity to work in concert with their peers for a common good.

School Community Problem-Solving

Inviting students to solve school community problems helps them see that teachers and staff value them as contributors, not just learners. Topeka superintendent Tiffany Anderson created equity councils made up of staff and students at each school in her district. We talked with Dr. Anderson, who explains,

> [T]hose students were given opportunities to look at patterns and trends within their own schools, desegregated by color and gender, and to question why there are patterns that might be indicating that we have some greater problems, such as seeing that some students are not selecting the highest-level courses when it is clear that they have an aptitude for AP (advanced placement) courses, but they are not selecting that. We ask ourselves why. And sometimes we come up with an answer that may make us all uncomfortable, which might include that students choose not to challenge themselves because they do not feel they are going to get a fair opportunity, which again, that

is a mindset. Students also brought up that the decision could be because of funding, so the AP test and the cost of that. So, we have eliminated that by using title funds, which we now have the flexibility to use, and we pay for all AP courses, the tests. We pay for all ACT tests to be taken during the school day. We really look at the challenges and barriers that are being put in place, but rather than us looking at it from an adult perspective, we are fostering and facilitating conversation among youth so that they really lead this dialogue, and we learn more from them than if we were leading the conversation ourselves absent of their voice.

The educators in Topeka are inviting students to collaborate on solving problems that matter to them and their peers. Notice that in this example the students are embedded in ongoing significant school problem-solving (and not pitching another school recycling plan). Of course, the challenge for this work is that if you invite students into these conversations, you must be committed to finding realistic solutions. This requires lots of individual and community work with restorative justice, but the rewards are hugely significant. (For resources on restorative justice, go to the Schott Foundation for Public Education's website [Schott Foundation for Public Education n.d.].) Dr. Anderson traces her 10 percent increase in graduation rates in one year to beginning to do this work. Students understood that their relationships with teachers and school staff went beyond a hierarchy of submission and dominance to a problem-solving partnership.

The Work of Relationships Is Ongoing

The work of building positive relationships with students is ongoing. *Ongoing* does not just mean that we try to make it happen every day but that we take responsibility for the times we do not quite measure up to our ideals. There are times, there will be times to come, when we get so worn down by life that we are not present in the way we want to be. In those times, we have to reenter relationships with humility. Most teachers describe having positive relationships with all their students, but what is the evidence of that? Has each student grown academically and personally that year? Have you changed your practice in response to learning from your students? A true relationship is a two-way dialogue and requires us to change behaviors and mindsets that diminish the other person. It is intense and intensely rewarding but it is not more than you can handle. Respect yourself. Take care of yourself. Be aware of how school can oppress some students so that you can disrupt that oppression. Learn from your students. And you will find great joy.

AFTERWORD

M. Colleen Cruz

There was a kid in the school where I taught who was infamous. He was a member of a family who was infamous in the school community as well. The details do not matter. But suffice it to say, our school was not an easy place for him to be. Year after year, teachers tangled with him, then threw up their hands and passed him on to the next teacher.

But one year that pattern stopped. He had been held over for failure to make enough academic progress in third grade, by a teacher whose reputation for being traditional and inflexible was long and storied. However, our principal made a move I never would have predicted. Rather than keeping that student with the same teacher, or another teacher who might have been less traditional but known for their academic urgency, she placed him with a teacher who was known for his laissez faire attitude, quirkiness, and general fondness for all kids.

The boy flourished in his class, and when the time came to pass him on to the next teacher, while the boy was still considered infamous, he was also developing a reputation for being charming and bright. The boy's teacher was given the latitude to choose the next teacher and he chose me. I distinctly remember my third-grade colleague handing me the boy's files and saying, "I love him. He can keep you on your toes, as can his mother. But make no mistake, he is a great kid. I chose you for his next teacher because I know you will love him too."

My colleague was right. On all counts. I did love this boy and he did keep my on my toes. If ever I found myself unsnarling a tangle we were in, and getting frustrated about it, I would remember my colleague's words and double down on my relationship with the boy. He made huge progress during the year he was in my class. When the year drew to a close, I too was given the choice of his teacher in the next grade. I chose a funny, relaxed colleague, who never met a kid he did not like. I handed the boy's folder over to him with the same message of "You will love this boy." And of course, my colleague adored the boy and the boy had a good year.

Years later, I got a message on Facebook from that same fifth-grade colleague. "Guess what? Our student just graduated from college and already has a job with the city. I feel so good about how he was passed from teacher to teacher who loved him. I think we helped to make a difference."

That student from many years ago, the one a string of three teachers loved and connected with, came right into my mind as I first read the book you now hold in your hands. Tyrone C. Howard, Jaleel R. Howard, and Tanya Milner-McCall have captured, both through research and practice, the kernel of what is at the center of transformative teaching: relationships. They explained when and how teachers can actively choose to prioritize their relationships with students and why this is not only important work— but *the* most important work.

I am incredibly grateful to the authors of this book for the powerful text they put together. I am particularly grateful to know that teachers all over, who have always believed in the importance of relationships with students, will find the backing and support they sought within the pages of this book.

REFERENCES

ABC News. n.d. "Teacher Has Personalized Handshakes with Every One of His Students." www.facebook.com/ABCNews /videos/10155345236708812/.

Ahmed, Sara K. 2018. *Being the Change: Lessons and Strategies to Teach Social Comprehension.* Portsmouth, NH: Heinemann.

Alliance for Excellence in Education. n.d. "The High Cost of High School Dropouts: The Economic Case for Reducing the High School Dropout Rate." https://all4ed.org/take-action/action -academy/the-economic-case-for-reducing-the-high-school -dropout-rate/.

Arellano, Adele, José Cintrón, Barbara Flores, and Margarita Berta-Ávila. 2016. "Teaching for Critical Consciousness: Topics, Themes, Frameworks, and Instructional Activities." In *Growing Critically Conscious Teachers*, edited by Angela Valenzuela, 39–66. New York, NY: Teachers College Press.

Barshay, Jill. 2019. "Research Scholars to Air Problems with Using 'Grit' at School." The Hechinger Report. https:// hechingerreport.org/research-scholars-to-air-problems-with -using-grit-at-school/.

Battistich, Victor, Eric Schaps, and Nance Wilson. 2004. "Effects of an Elementary School Intervention on Students' 'Connectedness' to School and Social Adjustment During Middle School." *The Journal of Primary Prevention* 24 (3): 243–62.

Berson, Ilene R., and Jennifer Baggerly. 2012. "Building Resilience to Trauma: Creating a Safe and Supportive Early Childhood Classroom." *Childhood Education* 85 (6): 375–79.

Birch, Sondra H., and Gary W. Ladd. 1997. "The Teacher-Child Relationship and Early School Adjustment." *Journal of School Psychology* 55 (1): 61–79.

Bright Tots. 2012. "Choosing the Right Educational Toys for Children." www.brighttots.com/domains.

Brown, Brené. 2012. *Daring Greatly: How the Courage to Be Vulnerable Transforms the Way We Live, Love, Parent, and Lead*. New York, NY: Avery.

Cherng, Hua-Yu Sebastian, and Peter F. Halpin. 2016. "The Importance of Minority Teachers' Student Perceptions of Minority Teachers." *Educational Research* 45 (7): 407–20.

Comer, James P. 1980, 1993. *School Power: Implications of an Intervention Project*. New York, NY: The Free Press.

Craig, Susan E. 2016. *Trauma-Sensitive Schools: Learning Communities Transforming Children's Lives, K–5*. New York, NY: Teachers College Press.

Curby, Timothy W., Jennifer LoCasale-Crouch, Timothy R. Konold, Robert C. Pianta, Carollee Howes, Margaret Burchinal, Donna Bryant, Richard Clifford, Diane Early, and Oscar Barbarin. 2009. "The Relations of Observed Pre-K Classroom Quality Profiles to Children's Achievement and Social Competence." *Early Education and Development* 20 (2): 346-372.

Darling-Hammond, Linda. 2010. *The Flat World and Education: How America's Commitment to Equity Will Determine Our Future*. New York, NY: Teachers College Press.

Davis, Mark H. 1994. *Empathy: A Social Psychological Approach*. Boulder, CO: Westview Press.

De Boer, Hester, Anneke C. Timmermans, and Margaretha P. C. Van Der Werf. 2018. "The Effects of Teacher Expectation Interventions on Teachers' Expectations and Student Achievement: Narrative Review and Meta-analysis." *Educational Research and Evaluation* 24: 3–5, 180–200.

Decker, Dawn M., Daria Paul Dona, and Sandra L. Christenson. 2007. "Behaviorally At-Risk African American Students: The Importance of Student-Teacher Relationships for Student Outcomes." *Journal of School Psychology* 45 (1): 83–109.

Downer, Jason T., Priscilla Goble, Sonya S. Myers, and Robert C. Pianta. 2016. "Teacher-Child Racial/Ethnic Match Within Pre-Kindergarten Classrooms and Children's Early School Adjustment." *Early Childhood Research Quarterly* 37: 26–38.

Duckworth, Angela. 2016. *Grit. The Power of Passion and Perseverance.* New York, NY: Simon & Schuster.

Dunbar, Robin. 2014. *Human Evolution: A Pelican Introduction.* New Orleans, LA: Pelican Books.

The EdCamp Foundation. 2014. *The Edcamp Model Powering Up Professional Learning.* Thousand Oaks, CA: Corwin.

Eisenberger, Naomi I., Matthew D. Lieberman, and Kipling D. Williams. 2003. "Does Rejection Hurt? An fMRI Study of Social Exclusion." *Science* 302: 290–92.

Ewing, Allison R., and Angela R. Taylor. 2009. "The Role of Child Gender and Ethnicity in Teacher-Child Relationship Quality and Children's Behavioral Adjustment in Preschool." *Early Childhood Research Quarterly* 24 (1): 92–105.

Felitti, Vincent J., Robert F. Anda, Dale Nordenberg, David F. Williamson, Alison M. Spitz, Valerie Edwards, Mary P. Koss, and James S. Marks. 1998. "Relationship of Childhood Abuse and Household Dysfunction to Many of the Leading Causes of Death in Adults: The Adverse Childhood Experiences (ACE) Study." *American Journal of Preventive Medicine* 14: 245–58.

Fryer, Roland G. Jr., 2018. "The 'Pupil' Factory: Specialization and the Production of Human Capital in Schools." *American Economic Review* 108 (3): 616–56.

Gaffney, Carrie. 2019. "When Schools Cause Trauma." *Teaching Tolerance* 62. www.tolerance.org/magazine/summer-2019/when-schools-cause-trauma.

Gaunt, Kyra D. 2006. *The Games Black Girls Play: Learning the Ropes from Double Dutch to Hip Hop.* New York, NY: University Press.

Gay, Geneva. 2010. *Culturally Responsive Teaching.* New York, NY: Teachers College Press.

———. 2018. *Culturally Responsive Teaching: Teaching, Research and Practice* 3rd ed. New York, NY: Teachers College Press.

Gershenson, Seth, Stephen B. Holt, and Nicholas Papageorge. 2016. "Who Believes in Me? The Effect of Student–Teacher Demographic Match on Teacher Expectations." *Economics of Education Review* 52: 209–24.

González, Norma, Luis C. Moll, and Cathy Amanti, eds. 2005. *Funds of Knowledge: Theorizing Practices in Households, Communities and Classrooms.* Mahwah, NJ: Erlbaum.

Gutiérrez, Kris D., and Barbara Rogoff. 2003. "Cultural Ways of Learning: Individual Traits of Repertoires of Practice." *Educational Research* 32 (5): 19–25.

Hammond, Zaretta L. 2015. *Culturally Responsive Teaching and the Brain: Promoting Authentic Engagement and Rigor Among Culturally and Linguistically Diverse Students.* Thousand Oaks, CA: Corwin Press.

Hamre, Bridget K., and Robert C. Pianta. 2001. "Early Teacher–Child Relationships and the Trajectory of Children's School Outcomes Through Eighth Grade." *Child Development* 72 (2): 625–638.

Henderson, Anne T., Karen L. Mapp, Vivian R. Johnson, and Don Davies. 2007. *Beyond the Bake Sale: The Essential Guide to Family-School Partnerships.* New York, NY: The New Press.

High Quality Project Based Learning. n.d. "A Framework for High Quality Project Based Learning." https://hqpbl.org/wp-content/uploads/2018/03/FrameworkforHQPBL.pdf.

Hill, Andrew J., and Daniel B. Jones. 2018. "A Teacher Who Knows Me: The Academic Benefits of Repeat Student-Teacher Matches." *Economics of Education Review* 64: 1–12.

Howard, Tyrone C. 2003. "Culturally Relevant Pedagogy: Ingredients for Critical Teacher Reflection." *Theory into Practice* 42 (3): 195–202.

———. 2020. *Why Race and Culture Matters in Schools: Closing the Achievement Gap in America's Classrooms* 2nd ed. New York, NY: Teachers College Press.

Johnston, Peter H. 2004. *Choice Words: How Our Language Affects Children's Learning.* Portland, ME: Stenhouse.

Klem, Adena M., and James P. Connell. 2004. "Relationships Matter: Linking Teacher Support to Student Engagement and Achievement." *Journal of School Health* 74 (7): 262-73.

Kohli, Rita. 2016. "Behind School Doors: The Impact of Hostile Racial Climates on Urban Teachers of Color." *Urban Education* 53 (3): 307–33.

Kohli, Rita, Bree Picower, Antonio Nieves Martinez, and Natalia Ortiz. 2015. "Critical Professional Development: Centering the Social Justice Needs of Teachers." *The International Journal of Critical Pedagogy* 6 (2): 7–24.

Kohli, Rita, and Daniel G. Solórzano. 2012. "Teachers, Please Learn Our Names!: Racial Microaggressions and the K–12 Classroom." *Race Ethnicity and Education* 15 (4): 441–462.

Ladson-Billings, Gloria. 1994. *The Dreamkeepers: Successful Teachers of African American Children.* San Francisco: Jossey-Bass, Inc.

———. 1995. "Toward a Theory of Culturally Relevant Pedagogy." *American Educational Research Journal* 32 (3): 465–491.

Lieberman, Matthew. 2013. *Social: Why Our Brains Are Wired to Connect.* New York, NY: Crown.

Locks, Angela. n.d. "Summary of Yosso's Cultural Wealth Model." https://smu.app.box.com/s/dvn2wkemz0rt65jodujtxt1qe5gniekv.

Love, Bettina. 2019. *We Want to Do More Than Survive: Abolitionist Teaching and the Pursuit of Educational Freedom.* Boston: Beacon Press.

Lynn, Marvin, and Adrienne D. Dixson. 2013. *Handbook of Critical Race Theory in Education.* New York, NY: Routledge.

McAllister, Gretchen, and Jacqueline Jordan Irvine. 2002. "The Role of Empathy in Teaching Culturally Diverse Students: A Qualitative Study of Teachers' Beliefs." *Journal of Teacher Education* 53 (5): 433–43.

Mehta, Jal. 2015. "The Problem with Grit." Harvard Graduate School of Education. www.gse.harvard.edu/news/15/04/problem-grit.

Miller, Richard M. 2008. *The Influence of Teachers' Caring Behaviors on High School Students' Behavior and Grades.* Seton Hall University Dissertations and Theses (ETDs). Paper 1633.

Milner, H. Richard, IV. 2010. *Start Where You Are, But Don't Stay There: Understanding Diversity, Opportunity Gaps, and Teaching in Today's Classrooms.* Cambridge, MA: Harvard Education Press.

———. 2015. *Rac(e)ing to Class: Confronting Poverty and Race in Schools and Classrooms.* Cambridge, MA: Harvard Education Press.

Moll, Luis C., Cathy Amanti, Deborah Neff, and Norma Gonzalez. 1992. "Funds of Knowledge for Teaching: Using a Qualitative Approach to Connect Homes and Classrooms." *Theory into Practice* 31 (2): 132–141.

National Center for Education Statistics. 2017. www.nces.ed.gov.

The National Center on Family Homelessness. www.air.org/center /national-center-family-homelessness.

Office of Superintendent of Public Instruction. Migrant and Bilingual Education. "Funds of Knowledge." www.k12 .wa.us/student-success/access-opportunity-education /migrant-and-bilingual-education/funds-knowledge-and -home-visits-toolkit-overview/funds-knowledge.

Paris, Django, and H. Samy Alim, eds. 2017. *Culturally Sustaining Pedagogies: Teaching and Learning for Justice in a Changing World.* Language and Literacy Series. New York, NY: Teachers College Press.

Pena, Robert A., and Audrey Amrein. 1999. "Classroom Management and Caring." *Teaching Education* 10 (2): 169–79.

Pérez Huber, Lindsay. 2018. "Racial Microaffirmations as a Response to Microaggressions." Center for Critical Race Studies at UCLA. Research briefs. Issue No. 15. University of California, Los Angeles.

Pérez Huber, Lindsay, and Daniel G. Solórzano. 2015. "Microaggressions: What They Are, What They Are Not, and Why They Matter." *Latino Policy & Issues Brief* 30: 1–4. UCLA Chicano Studies Research Center.

———. 2015. "Racial Microaggression as a Tool for Critical Race Research." *Race Ethnicity and Education* 18 (3): 297–320.

Pew Research Center, Hispanic Trends. 2015. "Modern Immigration Wave Brings 59 Million to U.S., Driving Population Growth and Change Through 2065: Views of Immigration's Impact on U.S. Society Mixed." Retrieved from www.pewresearch. org/hispanic/2015/09/28/modern-immigration-wave-brings -59-million-to-u-s-driving-population-growth-and-change -through-2065/www.perhisto-panic.org/2015/09/28.

Pierce, Chester. 1969. "Is Bigotry the Basis of the Medical Problem of the Ghetto?" In *Medicine in the Ghetto,* edited by J. Norman, 301–14. New York, NY: Meredith Corporation.

———. 1970. "Offensive Mechanisms." In *The Black Seventies,* edited by F. Barbour, 265–82. Boston, MA: Porter Sargent.

Powell, Candice, Cynthia Demetriou, and Annice Fisher. 2013. "Micro-affirmations in Academic Advising: Small Act, Big Impact." *The Mentor: An Academic Advising Journal* 15. https://dus.psu.edu/mentor/2013/10/839/.

Reynolds, Rema Ella, Tyrone C. Howard, and Tomashu Kenyatta Jones. 2015. "Is This What Educators Really Want? Transforming the Discourse on Black Fathers and Their Participation in Schools." *Race Ethnicity and Education* 18 (1): 89–107.

Rist, Ray C. 1970. "Student Social Class and Teacher Expectations: The Self-Fulfilling Prophecy in Ghetto Education." *Harvard Educational Review* 40 (3): 411–51.

Rowe, Mary. 2008. "Micro-Affirmations and Micro-Inequities." *Journal of the International Ombudsman Association* 1 (1): 45–48.

Rudasill, Kathleen Moritz, Kathleen Cranley Gallagher, and Jamie M. White. 2001. "Temperamental Attention and Activity, Classroom Emotional Support, and Academic Achievement in Third Grade." *Journal of School Psychology* 48 (2): 113–134.

Rudasill, Kathleen Moritz, Sara E. Rimm-Kaufman, Laura M. Justice, and Khara Pence. 2006. "Temperament and Language Skills as Predictors of Teacher–Child Relationship Quality in Preschool." *Early Education and Development* 17 (2): 271–91.

Schott Foundation for Public Education. n.d. "Restorative Practices: A Guide for Educators." http://schottfoundation.org/restorative-practices.

Shalaby, Carla. 2017. *Troublemakers: Lessons in Freedom from Young Children at School.* New York, NY: New Press.

Smith, Emily Esfahani. 2013. "Social Connection Makes a Better Brain." *The Atlantic.* October 19. www.theatlantic.com/health/archive/2013/10/social-connection-makes-a-better-brain/280934/.

Souto-Manning, Mariana, Carmen I. Lugo Llerena, Jessica Martell, Abigail Salas Maguire, and Alicia Arce-Boardman. 2018. *No More Culturally Irrelevant Teaching*. Portsmouth, NH: Heinemann.

Sparks, Sarah D. 2016. "Emotions Help Steer Students' Learning, Studies Find." *Education Week* 35 (29). www.edweek.org /ew/articles/2016/04/27/emotions-help-steer-students -learning-studies-find.html.

Stevenson, Howard C. 2014. *Promoting Racial Literacy in Schools: Differences That Make a Difference*. New York, NY: Teachers College Press.

Suárez-Orozco, Marcelo M., and M. Michikyan. 2016. "Introduction: Education for Citizenship in the Age of Globalization and Mass Migration." In *Global Migration, Diversity, and Civic Education*, edited by James A. Banks, Miriam Ben-Peretz, and Marcelo Suárez-Orozco, 1–25. New York, NY: Teachers College Press and The National Academy of Education.

Sue, Derald Wing. 2010. *Microaggressions in Everyday Life: Race, Gender and Sexual Orientation*. Hoboken, NJ: Wiley & Sons.

Tenenbaum, Harriet R., and Martin D. Ruck. 2007. "Are Teachers' Expectations Different for Racial Minority than for European American Students? A Meta-Analysis." *Journal of Educational Psychology* 99 (2): 253–73.

Teven, Jason J., and James C. McCroskey. 1997. "The Relationship of Perceived Teacher Caring with Student Learning and Teacher Evaluation." *Communications Education* 46: 1–9.

UCLA Diversity and Faculty Development. 2014. "Diversity in the Classroom." https://equity.ucla.edu/wp-content/uploads /2016/06/DiversityintheClassroom2014Web.pdf.

Ullucci, Kerri, and Dan Battey. 2011. "Exposing Colorblindness /Grounding Color Consciousness: Challenges for Teacher Education." *Urban Education* 46 (6): 1195–225.

U.S. Census Bureau. 2015. Retrieved from www.census.gov /programs-surveys/acs/guidance/comparing-acs-data/2015 .html on April 26, 2019.

U.S. Department of Education, Office of Planning, Evaluation and Policy Development, Policy and Program Studies Service. 2016. "The State of Racial Diversity in the Educator Workforce." Washington, D.C. www2.ed.gov/rschstat/eval /highered/racial-diversity/state-racial-diversity-workforce.pdf.

U.S. Department of Health and Human Services. "Facts About Bullying." StopBullying.gov, last reviewed June 10, 2019, www.stopbullying.gov/resources/facts#stats.

U.S. Department of Justice, Bureau of Justice Statistics, School Crime Supplement to the National Crime Victimization Survey, 2015. Lessne, Deborah, and Melissa Cidade. 2016. "Split-half Administration of the 2015 School Crime Supplement to the National Crime Victimization Survey: Methodology Report." NCES 2017-004. U.S. Department of Education, Washington, D.C. National Center for Education Statistics. http://nces.ed.gov/pubsearch.

Warren, Chezare A. 2015. "Conflict and Contradictions: Conceptions of Empathy and the Work of Good-Intentioned Early Career White Female Teachers." *Urban Education* 50 (5): 572–600.

———. 2018. "Empathy, Teacher Dispositions, and Preparation for Culturally Responsive Pedagogy." *Journal of Teacher Education* 69 (2): 169–83.

Weinberger, Andrea H., Misato Gbedemah, Antigona Martinez, Denis Nash, S. Galea, and Renee D. Goodwin. 2017. "Trends in Depression Prevalence in the USA from 2005 to 2015: Widening Disparities in Vulnerable Groups." *Psychological Medicine* 48 (8): 1308–15.

Yosso, Tara J. 2005. "Whose Culture Has Capital? A Critical Race Theory Discussion of Community Cultural Wealth." *Race Ethnicity and Education.* 8 (1): 69–91. www.tandfonline .com/doi/abs/10.1080/1361332052000341006.